Balanced Diversity

Also by Karen Ferris:
Game On! Change is Constant
Unleash the Resiliator Within—Resilience: A Handbook for Individuals
Unleash the Resiliator Within—Resilience: A Handbook for Leaders

Balanced Diversity

A Portfolio Approach to Organizational Change

REVISED EDITION

Using research by Dr. Stephanie Bertels, Lisa Papania and Daniel Papania
for the Network for Business Sustainability (www.nbs.net)

KAREN FERRIS

Balanced Diversity:
A Portfolio Approach to Organizational Change

Typeset by BookPOD

Disclaimer
The material in this book is general comment only and neither purports nor intends to be specific advice related to any particular reader. It does not represent professional advice and should not be relied on as the basis for any decision or action on any matter that it covers. To the maximum extent permitted by law, the author and publisher disclaim all responsibility and liability to any person or entity, whether a purchaser or not, in respect to anything and of the consequences of anything done by any such person in reliance, whether in whole or in part, upon the whole or any part of the contents of this publication.

ISBN: 978-0-6484694-7-6 (pbk) eISBN: 978-0-6484694-8-3

 A catalogue record for this
book is available from the
National Library of Australia

About the Author

Karen Ferris is an unashamed organizational change management rebel with a cause. She likes to challenge the status quo but only when her reason for doing so is defensible.

Karen began her working life in IT but she has spent a large part of her career in the IT service management space where she is recognized globally for her expertise and insight.

As someone who is continually focused on the people side of change, Karen authored a publication titled *Balanced Diversity: A Portfolio Approach to Organizational Change* in 2010.

She considered herself an accidental author back then. She stumbled across a framework for embedding change, set out to write a white paper about it and ended up with a book. That was the moment she was propelled into the world of organizational change management.

In 2019, she published her second book *Game On! Change is Constant: Tactics to Win When Leading Change is Everyone's Business*. Karen is a sought after international keynote speaker, coach, mentor, facilitator and trainer.

Born in Liverpool, UK, she emigrated to Australia in 1998. She lives with her wife, Breed, in Melbourne. She is an avid Liverpool Football Club supporter, an Elvis fan, has an obsession with shoes, and is a self-confessed arctophile—you might want to Google that.

Acknowledgments

I would gratefully like to acknowledge those who have been key in helping me revise this book.

My first thank-you has to go to Dr. Stephanie Bertels. Without Dr. Bertels support, this publication, and the previous one, would not exist. I have to acknowledge the astounding work that Dr. Bertels and her research team undertook in creating the framework that forms the core of this publication; therefore, my thanks also go to her team at Simon Fraser University: Daniel and Lisa Papania.

A big thank-you goes to the team at Bison Creative for their excellent work on the graphics.

I am exceedingly grateful to Kirstie Magowan, for her help and guidance with the original edition of this publication.

Finally, I give my heartfelt thanks to my wife Breed for her continued support and encouragement throughout my writing journey and for encouraging me to put pen to paper once again to create the revised edition of this publication.

Contents

Preface

When this book was first written back in 2011, organizational change management (OCM) was very different.

Most of the methodologies, models, frameworks and approaches to OCM were based on the premise that Kurt Lewin—a German-American psychologist—supposedly said change could be accomplished in three steps:

unfreeze – transition – refreeze

Many of the methodologies, models, frameworks and approaches to OCM continue to be based on this premise. Research has shown, however, that Lewin never actually said such a thing.[1] Despite this fact, organizational change management has traditionally perceived change as a linear process.

The suggested scenario was that unfreeze was the phase in which there was preparation for change, transition was the phase in which there was a move forward to a new way of being and refreeze was the establishment of stability once the change had been made.

There is no stability anymore.

Today we are in a world in which change is constant. It is often described using the acronym VUCA:

> **Volatile**: constant and significant.
> **Uncertain**: unpredictable events and outcomes.
> **Complex**: many interconnected parts and variables.
> **Ambiguous**: lack of clarity—no precedents and unknown unknowns.

Change occurs faster and faster, and is less predictable and more disruptive. It is not linear and we no longer have those suggested periods of stability i.e. refreeze.

Therefore, the traditional methodologies, models, frameworks and approaches no longer meet the needs of this environment.

In the first edition of this book, I embedded the Balanced Diversity framework into a structured OCM methodology, which I now believe is outdated. So, the first major change to this edition is the approach I describe to applying the Balanced Diversity framework while managing change.

I have also moved the description of the approach and how to use the framework to the front of the publication, as the approach is just as important as the practices chosen from the Balanced Diversity framework. I have found that some of my readers have embraced the framework and the practices it contains but have not applied it in the most effective manner or in the manner intended. Therefore, it made sense to describe the approach before describing the framework in detail.

The second major change is that the Balanced Diversity framework practices are now described in the context of any change being made in any organization. The first edition focused on the application of the practices in the IT service management industry, as that was my target audience at the time and also the community of the commissioner (*it*SMF International) and the publisher (TSO).

This edition is targeted to a much wider audience—everybody.

Objective

The objective of this publication is to present a framework that enables organizations to successfully transition people through change. This objective has not changed since the first edition.

The focus, however, is more on using the practices to build resilience to change within the organization as opposed to overcoming resistance to change.

The Balanced Diversity framework is a reference guide for every leader of change who needs access to a wide range of practices.

The fundamental difference between this framework and others is that it advocates a balanced approach. The practices within the framework are arranged into groups (quadrants) of informal and formal practices that either deliver on current commitments (fulfillment) or move the organization further along the path to change (innovation).

The key is to select a balance of practices from each group in order to successfully embed change into the organization—just as we should select a balance of foods from each of the food groups for a healthy diet. This healthy change becomes part of the DNA of the organization.

Introduction

Overview and purpose

There are many changes to which this framework can be applied to ensure successful transitions to a desired state.

The framework can be applied to a waterfall, agile or hybrid project-driven change. It can also be used to build resilience in the face of constant change across the entire organization.

Tome after tome has been written about change initiatives failing to achieve a return on investment because they did not gain traction or become embedded as the new way of working. This publication proposes that the reason for the failure of these endeavors is the lack of a balanced approach using a diversity of practices to successfully transition to a desired state.

For example, many organizations will introduce a training program and some form of communication in the hope that the transition will be achieved. In most cases, this does not happen.

The reason is that those practices of training and communication are not diverse enough and do not provide a balanced portfolio of activities (or 'practices' as they will be referred to throughout this publication) for the transition to be successful.

The framework presented here provides a wide-ranging and diverse set of practices that can be used for successful transitions. The key is that they have been divided into informal and formal practices. They have then been grouped into those that will help the organization deliver on current commitments (referred to as fulfillment) and those that will help the organization move further along the path to change (referred to as innovation).

The result is that the framework provides four groups (quadrants) of practices from which leaders of change need to select a balanced portfolio of practices to make their transition a success. Practices need to be selected from each quadrant and used together to achieve sufficient penetration and traction to achieve the desired outcomes.

The framework should be an essential component within the toolkit of all change leaders and practitioners. It should be used as a reference guide for every organizational transition.

The framework can be used for any type of transition: strategic, tactical or operational, and in any industry vertical and in any size of organization.

This publication will introduce the framework and how it was constructed and provide guidance on how change leaders can use it to adopt a portfolio approach to transition.

Each of the quadrants of the framework, the categories and the individual practices are explored in detail.

There are 59 practices described, as per the original research. Additional commentary, based on my own knowledge, experience and research, is provided to expand the subject matter.

Each practice is accompanied by guidance to assist in its application.

It concludes with practical, case-study type examples of how the framework could be used for both new change initiatives and for existing change initiatives that are not having the desired adoption across the organization. It also has an example of how the framework can be used to improve resilience in the workforce.

This publication is not, and was never, one that explores organizational change management dynamics and transitions. It is intended be a reference text to which change leaders can turn when leading change to select a balanced portfolio of practices that will make the change a success.

The framework

In 2005, the Network for Business Sustainability (NBS) was established. NBS is a Canadian non-profit group that produces authoritative resources on important sustainability issues. In 2010, it commissioned a large-scale systematic review of both academic and practitioner resources related to embedding sustainability into organizational culture.

The research team, led by Dr. Stephanie Bertels, identified 13,756 academic and practitioner articles and reports related to the topic. A detailed review then narrowed this down to the most relevant 179 to be included in the systematic review. (Bertels, Papania, & Papania, 2010)

The extensive analysis of these sources revealed a multitude of ways that organizations can work to embed sustainability into organizational culture. In the end, the research team identified 59 distinct practices and grouped them in way that they anticipated would be meaningful to businesses.

The research, *Embedding Sustainability in Organizational Culture*, can be accessed at www.nbs.net.

The research team comprised:

> Dr. Stephanie Bertels, Faculty of Business, Simon Fraser University
> Lisa Papania, PhD candidate, Simon Fraser University
> Daniel Papania, PhD student, Simon Fraser University
> with research assistance by Sara Graves.

In 2011, as a result of my interest in sustainability for IT, I came across this body of research, and I soon realized it had far-reaching implications for those of us leading change.

Although the focus of the research was on embedding sustainability into organizational culture, my examination of the research results clearly showed that the findings could be related to embedding *any* type of change into organizational culture. *This publication* describes the framework and the practices within the framework, and how they each can be related to *all change initiatives*.

On discovering this research, I contacted NBS to request permission to reference the material in a white paper that I was keen to write as I knew I had uncovered something that was going to transform the way we look at introducing changes related to IT service management into our organizations.

Having been kindly given permission, I soon returned to ask whether that permission would be transferable to a book. The white paper evolved far more than I had intended as my excitement about the research application to IT service management continued to grow.

NBS put me in touch with Dr. Stephanie Bertels to whom I am eternally grateful for her willingness to allow me to use the framework.

The first publication presented the framework as detailed in the original research and demonstrated its practical application to *IT service management*. This publication presents the framework as detailed in the original research and demonstrates its practical application in relation to *any industry*.

When reading this, leaders of change can select from the 59 diverse practices within the framework to ensure they have a balanced approach to change. It will equip them with a balanced portfolio for success.

Intended audience

This publication is aimed at anyone trying to lead and drive change within the organization and transition the organization from a current state to a desired state.

You could be a change leader, HR professional, manager or change management professional or practitioner. You could be a change leader trying to move away from managing programs of change to building a platform for change and establishing change resilience within the organization.

The audience will comprise anyone who needs access to a practical and pragmatic approach to change and transitions.

The publication is intended to be a reference guide for practices that can be applied when change and transitions are needed.

I recommend you don't keep this to yourself but share it across your organization, as its application is widespread.

The challenge and solution

Challenge

It is not my intent to dive into the reasons why organizational change is a challenge. We know it is a challenge because it involves people, and everyone is different. Also, every organization is different with different goals and directions.

Our workforce is dynamic and will change over time in regard to demographics, geographical construct, and diversity etc. It is for this reason that a one-size-fits-all approach to change and transitions does not work.

All too often, organizations believe that a well-structured and planned-out program of communication will achieve the desired outcomes. This is often not the case.

The same applies to the provision of a program of training in relation to a particular change or transition. Training alone will not achieve the desired outcome.

Case study

As already mentioned, the original publication focused on the use of the framework in the IT service management profession.

As a result, I have worked with many IT departments to assist them to embed change into the organization and I have used the Balanced Diversity framework initially as an assessment tool.

I capture the practices currently in use to embed change within the organization and then determine the balance or imbalance. Once a baseline is established, I work with the organization to create a balanced portfolio of practices for a particular change initiative.

Without exception, in the many applications of this approach, all of the practices being used by IT have been formal practices to deliver on current commitment. The practices are all located in the top right-hand quadrant of the model.

The following diagram illustrates what that looks like.

Note: The diagram is a representation of the imbalance and it is not intended to be read in detail. The diagram is expanded on later in this publication.

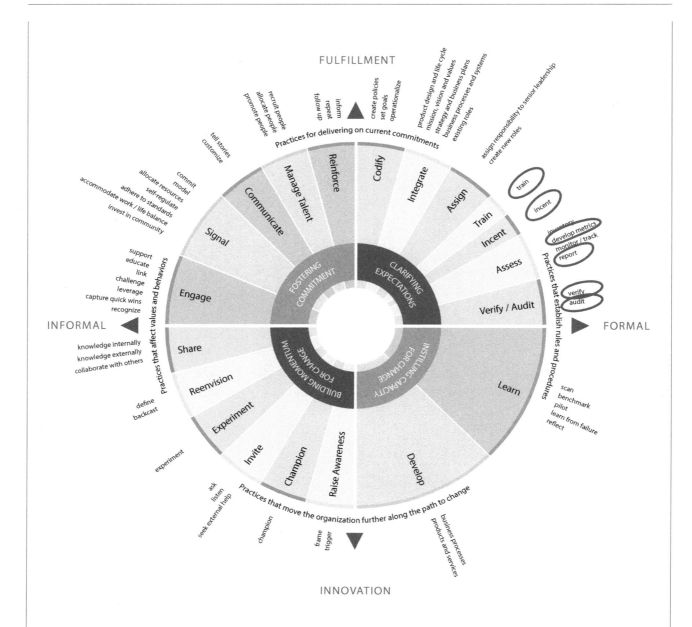

Figure 1: Example of IT practice selection for change

IT by nature likes to draw on formal activities such as training, providing incentives for adherence to processes, and developing metrics for process measurement and reporting upon them accordingly. It also has a strong tendency toward audits of processes, technology and systems, followed by a verification of those findings.

As can be seen, there is a vast imbalance. There are no informal activities selected (left side of framework) or activities that drive innovation (bottom of framework).

This imbalance is the reason why so many IT initiatives fail to gain momentum and deliver desired outcomes.

Solution

What is needed is a diverse set of practices and a balanced approach. The Balanced Diversity framework we will explore contains 59 practices for successful change or transitions.

Subsequent sections of this publication describe the framework, its construction and its application within the organization. The framework is structured in such a way that it allows for practices to be selected from four quadrants.

The key is for the selection to be balanced across all four quadrants. This provides a portfolio approach to organizational change and transition. The portfolio will include formal and informal practices that deliver on current change commitments and move the organization further along the path to future change initiatives.

It is this diverse yet balanced set of practices that will enable changes and transitions to be successful.

Before we look in detail at the framework, it is important that we first look at how it should be applied.

Application

The Balanced Diversity framework can be used for changes of any shape and size. It can be used for operational, tactical and strategic changes. It can be used in various delivery approaches including waterfall projects, agile project or hybrid approaches. It can be used on initiatives to increase resilience in the workforce.

It can be used on small, medium or large initiatives and changes.

Some pre-work must be done before selecting the practices from the framework.

It is imperative that the nature of the change or transition to be achieved is understood, the characteristic of the organization is known and the potential reaction to the change or transition by those impacted is recognized.

This information will ensure that the right practices are selected from the framework to address the challenges that may be faced.

Without this information, the tendency may be to choose practices with which you are comfortable and that are easily implemented. But the selected practices may not address the needs of the organization.

In this publication, it is not my intent to replicate organizational change management approaches. Rather I will provide guidance on the information you need to inform your selection process. How you obtain that information will be determined by the approach you are using.

For example, you will need to determine who your stakeholders are and their position in relation to a change to inform the choice of practices. This could be obtained through detailed stakeholder analysis, power / interest mapping, user stories and personas, discussions with a change alliance or a combination of these activities.

You will need to determine the characteristic of the organization in regard to change. Is the organization highly change resistant or does it embrace change?

This could be determined through surveys, workshops, cultural assessments, interviews or a combination of these activities.

You will need to determine the attributes of a change. Is it small, medium or large? Is it simple or complex? Who is impacted and are they all impacted in the same way? Is this a structure change, technology change, process change, people change or a combination of all four?

You may need to determine the level of resilience across the organization. Again, this could be determined through surveys, workshops, cultural assessments, interviews or a combination of these activities.

Is there high or low resilience? Are there pockets of resilience and where are they?

When you are equipped with this information, you can proceed with selection of the practices.

Select the practices

The information you need to select the practices includes, but does not have to be limited to, the following:

1. Stakeholders
2. Organizational characteristics
3. Change attributes
4. Levels of resilience.

You could also have a problem or opportunity statement, change definition and force field analysis, outputs from stand-ups, retrospectives and other ceremonies.

The more information you can gather, the better your selection of practices will be.

There are many ways in which you can select the practices. I recommend you workshop the selection with two or more people. Select people who have an interest in the change and brainstorm the practices.

Remember, the objective is to get a balance across each of the quadrants. It does not have to be a perfect balance but an overutilization of practices in one quadrant will not deliver the results you are seeking.

Here is a suggested workshop outline:

1. Share the information you have collected.
2. Furnish each participant with an A3 copy of the Balanced Diversity framework.
3. If the participants are not familiar with the framework, you may wish to commence with a presentation to introduce them to it and the concepts behind it.
4. Remind everyone that the aim is to get a balance of practices across the framework.
5. Illustrate the difference between a balanced selection and an unbalanced selection.

FULFILLMENT

INFORMAL

FORMAL

INNOVATION

Figure 2: Unbalanced selection

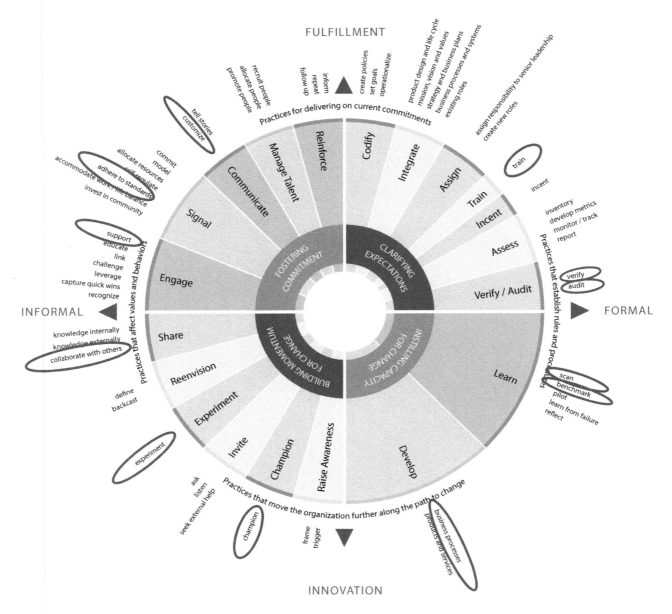

Figure 3: Balanced selection

6. If possible, project the framework onto a whiteboard, which can then be written upon.

7. As practices are selected, they can be circled and an ongoing check of balance can be made.

8. Questions to ask to guide selection of practices could include:

- Will this practice help solve the problem or address the opportunity?
- Does this practice reflect the stakeholder behaviors and positioning?
- Does this practice reflect the characteristics of the organization?
- Does this practice reflect the attributes of the change?
- Does this practice recognize the level of resilience?
- Will this practice help bring about the change we wish to see?
- Will this practice increase employee resilience?
- Have we selected too many or too few practices?

- Do we have the time?
- Do we have the skills?
- Do we have the resources?

9. Once the practices have been selected, check the following:

- There is a **balanced selection of practices from each quadrant**.
- There is the capability and capacity to deliver all of the selected practices in the time allowed.

10. Revise the selection until the above criteria can be met.

Roles and responsibilities

Once the selection of practices has been agreed upon, create a responsible, accountable, consulted and informed matrix (RACI) for each of the practices:

- Determine who will be accountable for its delivery.
- Determine who will be responsible for its delivery.
- Determine who will need to be consulted and when.
- Determine who will need to be informed and when.
- Define key milestones and delivery dates.
- Agree on the implementation approach.
- Agree on the target completion dates.

Document and distribute the outputs from the workshop.

Plan-Do-Check-Act

We cannot just assume, despite however much work we have put in, that the practices from the framework will continue to have the desired effect. The environment in which we are working is not static. It is constantly evolving and shifting and, therefore, the criteria on which we initially based our selection of practices may have changed also.

We need to check in to ensure that the desired effect is occurring and, if it's not, we need to take corrective action.

Just as with any process, the Balanced Diversity framework and the choice of practices should be subject to continual improvement. The Plan-Do-Check-Act (PDCA) framework is a simple but effective approach to continual improvement.

Dr. W Edwards Deming, a quality management authority, made the PDCA framework popular in the 1950s. It was originally developed by Walter Shewhart, a pioneering statistician who developed statistical process control in the Bell Laboratories in the USA during the 1930s.

Often now referred to as the Deming cycle or wheel, Deming himself always referred to it as the Shewhart cycle. PDCA was modified to Plan-Do-Study-Act, later in Deming's career as the word 'study' had closer meaning in English to the intent of Shewhart's word 'check'.

The PDCA framework is a four-stage approach to improvement as shown in Figure 4: The Deming cycle.

Figure 4: The Deming cycle

PLAN: Determine what needs to be improved. Gather data. Ask questions.

DO: Implement the solution—on a small scale, if possible—to test possible effects. Begin analysis.

CHECK: Monitor and review the change. Measure and compare results with expected results to determine any differences.

ACT: Make any required changes. Fully implement and embed. Embark on the next cycle of improvement.

In the context of the Balanced Diversity framework, we can use the PDCA cycle in the following manner:

Plan

Each time we utilize the framework, we will commence with planning and determine which practices we will choose from the framework.

Do

We will then implement the practices having ensured we have the capability and capacity to undertake all of the practices chosen. We will also clearly define the roles and responsibilities including time frames for the implementation of each of the practices.

Check

Now we need to check that they are having the desired effect. We can do this through observation, listening, surveys, face-to-face meetings, workshops, discussion groups, town hall meetings, feedback channels or even watercooler discussions. We can also look at metrics and measurements to determine if the change is succeeding.

Act

Where the desired effect is not being achieved, we need to determine why and address the gap.

Once we have determined the reason, we can make adjustments to the choice of practices or to the implementation approach for the chosen practices.

Having made the adjustments, we can commence with the planning stage once again.

The change curve

Understanding the emotional cycle that people will undergo and knowing the nature of your organization and its employees may also influence the practices you choose to employ from the framework. It will also help identify any changes to the practices you have chosen if you are not getting the desired results.

The change curve is a widely used model for understanding how people respond to change. There are many variations, but they are based on the Kübler-Ross model commonly known as the 'grief cycle', which psychiatrist Elisabeth Kübler-Ross introduced in her book *On Death and Dying*.

Her five-stage theory sought to explain how people dealt with catastrophic personal loss such as death or being diagnosed with a terminal illness. It was later recognized that this theory also applied to how people responded to any major change and the change curve resulted.

The stages are denial, anger, bargaining, depression and acceptance.

There is debate as to whether everyone goes through all of the stages on the curve. For example, some people may embrace change and go straight to acceptance and not experience the preceding stages. This, however, will depend on the nature of the change and how it affects each individual.

The thing to remember is that you are likely to have people at every stage of the change curve and you cannot rush to the next change just because you have a handful of people in the acceptance stage. You need to recognize where everyone is on the curve and work to bring them all to acceptance. It is also important to remember that people can move up and down the change curve—it is not a one-way street.

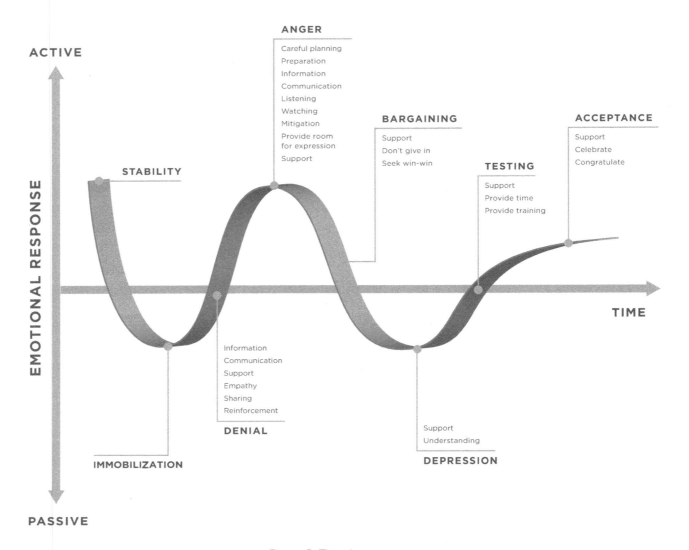

Figure 5: The change curve

The change curve shows the five stages on the roller-coaster ride of emotions related to a change that Kübler-Ross described, plus some extensions. It also notes the responses that can be made to individuals who are in that stage of the change curve.

It is important to note that the length and depth of each phase will be different for each person. Some people may spend a long time in the depression stage albeit not deeply entrenched in it; therefore, that part of the curve will be elongated and shallower for them than for others. Some people may go into a period of deep depression but come out of it quickly; therefore, that part of the curve for them will be short in length but deep in penetration.

Before the cycle starts, there is a period of stability where everything is fine and the employee is comfortable in their situation. Then the change is introduced or announced. There may be a period of immobilization. This is where there is fear and confusion and employees may even be overwhelmed by the perceived impact of the change on them.

Denial

> **"** There is no need to change. The way
> we do things now is just fine. **"**

> **"** It is just another fad and it simply won't happen. **"**

This is the stage where the reality of the change is felt and this results in denial. The response is to ignore the fact that the change has been announced and to carry on as if nothing has happened.

Response: The provision of information and good communication is essential at this stage. Regular communication regarding the change, the reason for the change and where employees can go to get more information and support is needed. Make sure the communication channels are open but don't overwhelm employees with vast amounts of information all at one time. Deliver information in a piecemeal fashion and provide the ability for employees to obtain more information as and when they want it.

People can be moved from denial into anger through empathy. Share their fears and resentment, and encourage them to air how they feel while reinforcing the message that the change IS going to happen.

Practices: Two practices from each quadrant that may be considered for selection from the framework at this stage include (but are not limited to):

Quadrant		Category	Practice
Clarifying expectations		Assign	Assign responsibility to senior leadership
		Assess	Inventory
Fostering commitment		Reinforce	Inform
		Engage	Support
Instilling capacity for change		Learn	Learn from failure
			Reflect
Building momentum for change		Invite	Ask
			Listen

Table 1: Suggested practices for denial stage

Note: These are suggestions only and should not remove the need for careful planning and selection of practices.

Anger

> **❝** Why me? It's not fair! Who is to blame
> for this? Why not you? **❞**

This is the stage where the emotional outpouring occurs and needs careful management to avoid crisis or chaos. At this stage, people look for someone to blame and express anger at those they perceive not to be impacted by the change.

Response: Careful planning for this stage is required. It is necessary to have considered what the impacts of the change will be on people and what objections they may have. This should be reflected in the communication and information being provided so that the objections can be mitigated as early as possible. Of course, there will be responses that could not have been foreseen so it is important to listen to what is being said and watch what is happening so that mitigating action can take place in a timely manner.

It is also important to allow employees to express their anger as long as it does not become destructive. Provide support and opportunities for them to air their grievances. Lack of response at this stage can result in a move back into the denial stage.

Practices: Two practices from each quadrant that may be considered for selection from the framework at this stage include (but are not limited to):

Quadrant	Category	Practice
Clarifying expectations	Assign	Assign responsibility to senior leadership
		Create new roles
Fostering commitment	Communicate	Tell stories
	Signal	Commit
Instilling capacity for change	Learn	Learn from failure
		Reflect
Building momentum for change	Invite	Ask
		Listen

Table 2: Suggested practices for anger stage

Note: These are suggestions only and should not remove the need for careful planning and selection of practices.

Bargaining

❝I'll do a different job.❞

❝Can't you wait a while?❞

In this stage, it is recognized that the change is going to happen; therefore, bargaining activities come into play to try to postpone or delay the change and its impact on the individual. It is a vain attempt to avoid the change at all costs.

Bargaining could include employees seeking an alternative position within the organization that they perceive will not be impacted by the change or trying to negotiate a partial adoption of the change. Employees will talk about their tenure, loyalty, performance records etc. to support their bargaining.

Response: The key here is to provide support and not agree to anything that cannot be provided. If there are opportunities for a win-win situation (where something can be offered to the employee in exchange for support of the change), they should be explored.

Practices: Two practices from each quadrant that may be considered for selection from the framework at this stage include (but are not limited to):

Quadrant	Category	Practice
Clarifying expectations	Assign	Assign responsibility to senior leadership
		Create new roles
Fostering commitment	Communicate	Tell stories
	Engage	Support
Instilling capacity for change	Learn	Learn from failure
		Reflect
Building momentum for change	Raise Awareness	Frame
		Trigger

Table 3: Suggested practices for bargaining stage

Note: These are suggestions only and should not remove the need for careful planning and selection of practices.

Depression

"What's the point?"

"Why bother?"

This is the stage where the certainty of the change is realised; this results in reluctant acceptance.

Depression sets in and employees turn in toward themselves, refusing any help or support from others. Everything seems black and desolate. This stage may manifest through a rise in absenteeism, sick leave, poor performance and poor punctuality etc.

Response: The best response at this stage is support and understanding. It is important that employees do not feel alone and know that support is readily available and forthcoming.

Practices: Two practices from each quadrant that may be considered for selection from the framework at this stage include (but are not limited to):

Quadrant	Category	Practice
Clarifying expectations	Assign	Assign responsibility to senior leadership
		Existing roles
Fostering commitment	Signal	Commit
	Communicate	Customize
Instilling capacity for change	Learn	Benchmark
		Pilot
Building momentum for change	Raise Awareness	Frame
		Trigger

Table 4: Suggested practices for depression stage

Note: These are suggestions only and should not remove the need for careful planning and selection of practices.

Testing

> **"** OK, maybe I'll listen. **"**

> **"** What's in it for me? **"**

In this stage, there is a move out of depression as the realization that the change is going to happen occurs. Employees now explore change and try new options to see if they can make the new way work for them. This is a period of exploration and learning. This is also the turning point for the organization and the individual.

Response: Give employees support to explore and test what the change means to them. Ensure that enough time is provided to allow this to happen fully. Provide training for employees so that they are well prepared for the change. Build in time to the day-to-day activities to allow for learning and exploration. Don't expect this to happen as an addition to business as usual.

Practices: Two practices from each quadrant that may be considered for selection from the framework at this stage include (but are not limited to):

Quadrant		Category	Practice
Clarifying expectations		Train	Train
		Integrate	Existing roles
Fostering commitment		Engage	Educate
			Recognize
Instilling capacity for change		Learn	Scan
			Pilot
Building momentum for change		Champion	Champion
		Experiment	Experiment

Table 5: Suggested practices for testing stage

Note: These are suggestions only and should not remove the need for careful planning and selection of practices.

Acceptance

> **"** It's going to be okay. **"**

This stage is where the individual accepts that the change is happening and finds a way forward. They take responsibility for their actions. Acceptance may initially be a resistant acceptance, but it will become a positive acceptance over time.

Response: At this stage, ongoing support is required for those who have been impacted by the change and may have found themselves in new roles or have changed roles within the organization. The key is to celebrate the success.

Congratulate individuals for getting through the change process and celebrate the successful implementation of the change as an organization. Involve everyone as this celebration of success is going to make the implementation of the next change easier.

Practices: Two practices from each quadrant that may be considered for selection from the framework at this stage include (but are not limited to):

Quadrant	Category	Practice
Clarifying expectations	Incent	Incent
	Assess	Develop metrics
Fostering commitment	Reinforce	Follow up
	Signal	Model
Instilling capacity for change	Learn	Learn from failure
		Reflect
Building momentum for change	Share	Knowledge internally
		Knowledge externally

Table 6: Suggested practices for acceptance stage

Note: These are suggestions only and should not remove the need for careful planning and selection of practices.

The framework

The framework revolves around two main dimensions relating to intent and approach. Intent is what you are trying to accomplish. Approach is how you are going to do it.

Intent: what you are trying to accomplish

On the path to making a change, organizations face tensions between ensuring they meet existing commitments (fulfillment) and making way for changes that will help them improve performance in the long term (innovation). These two goals form the vertical axis of the framework.

FULFILLMENT

INNOVATION

Figure 6: Vertical axis

Fulfillment: These are practices targeted at delivering on current commitments or implementing current initiatives. These practices involve discussion about what the organization 'should do' and emphasize compliance, operational excellence and targeted reinforcement, or refining what the organization is already doing in the area of the intended change.

Innovation: These are practices aimed at innovation: looking at better or different ways to do things. These practices involve discussion about what the organization 'could do' and involve experimenting, listening and trying new things.

Approach: how you are going to do it

There are two different approaches to embedding change: informal and formal.

There is an ongoing interplay between these approaches and both impact culture.

This requires management awareness of the impact of both hard and soft approaches to building cultural change.

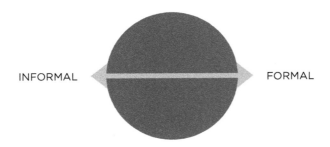

Figure 7: Horizontal axis

Informal: The informal approaches to shaping an organization's culture target people's values as well as social norms. A social norm is an expectation that people will behave in a certain way.

Norms (as opposed to rules) are enforced by other members of the organization through the use of social sanction. Norms and values are generally passed on and shaped through observation or experience.

Thus, informal approaches aim to establish and reinforce shared values and shared ways of doing things that align the organization with its journey toward the intended change. This is often accomplished through discussion and   experiences, and by modeling desired behaviors.

Formal: Formal approaches to shaping an organization's culture try to guide behavior through the rules, systems and procedures. The idea is to codify and organize values and behaviors that have developed informally.

This is often accomplished by generating documents and texts such as codes of conduct, procedures, systems and training materials and by implementing programs.

The resulting four quadrants, as shown in Figure 8: Framework quadrants, represent the different types of practices that can be employed to embed change into the organizational culture.

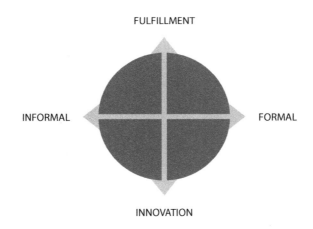

Figure 8: Framework quadrants

The 59 practices identified by the research are grouped into 20 categories across the four quadrants and the categories are shown in Figure 9: Framework categories.

Figure 9: Framework categories (Bertels, Papania, & Papania, 2010)

The 59 practices across each category are shown in the following diagram.

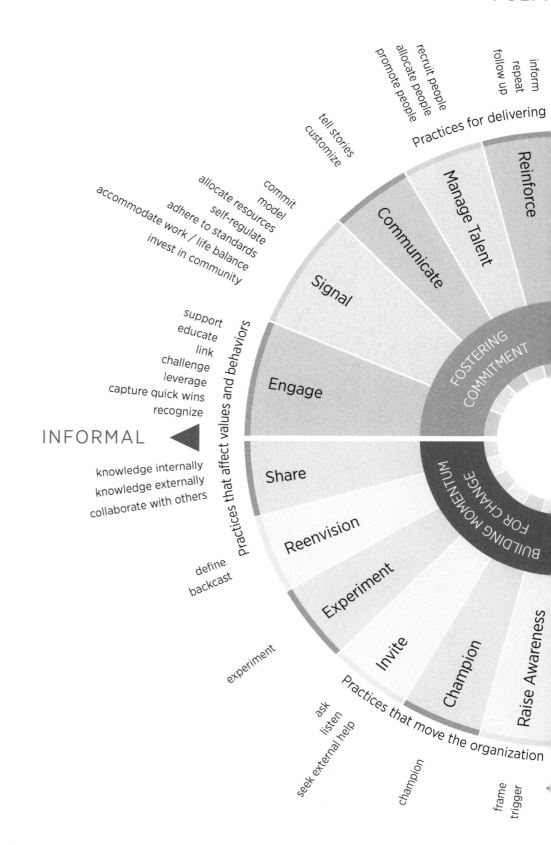

Figure 10: Framework practices (Bertels, Papania, & Papania, 2010)

MENT

create policies
set goals
operationalize

product design and life cycle
mission, vision and values
strategy and business plans
business processes and systems
existing roles

on current commitments

assign responsibility to senior leadership
create new roles

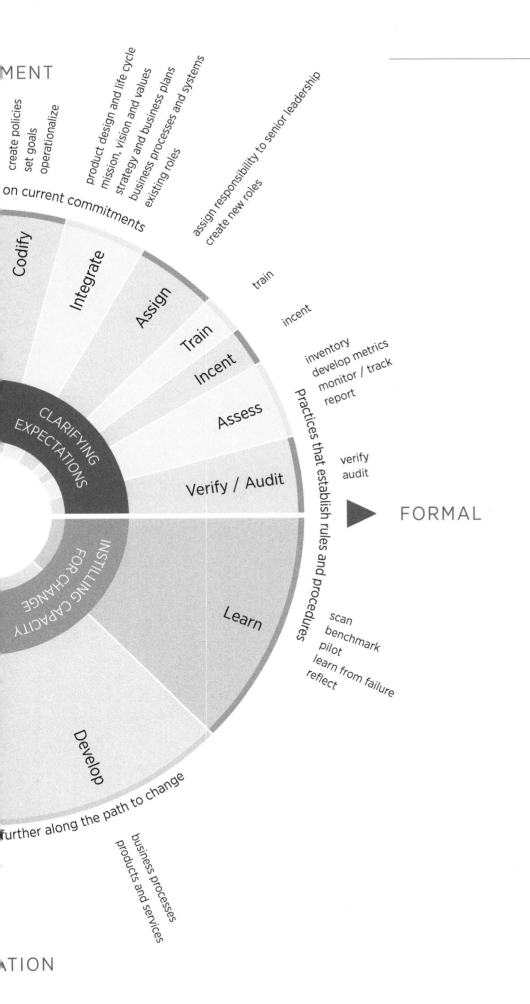

Codify

Integrate

Assign

Train

Incent

Assess

Verify / Audit

CLARIFYING
EXPECTATIONS

INSTILLING
CAPACITY
FOR CHANGE

Learn

Develop

train

incent

inventory
develop metrics
monitor / track
report

verify
audit

Practices that establish rules and procedures

▶ FORMAL

scan
benchmark
pilot
learn from failure
reflect

further along the path to change

business processes
products and services

ATION

The quadrant that depicts informal practices aimed at fulfillment is called **fostering commitment.**

Practices in this quadrant aim to build and reinforce the importance of the change for the organization, and to support and encourage those who are making efforts to embed the change.

There are five categories of practices: engaging, signaling, communicating, managing talent and reinforcing.

The quadrant that depicts the formal practices aimed at fulfillment is called **clarifying expectations**.

The practices in this quadrant aim to integrate the change into the core of the organization's strategies and processes; equip and encourage employees via training and incentives; and measure, track and report on the organization's progress.

There are seven categories of practices: codifying, integrating, assigning responsibility, training, incenting, assessing and verifying / auditing.

The quadrant that depicts the informal practices aimed at innovation is called **building momentum for change**.

The practices in this quadrant aim to support a culture of change innovation by developing the new ideas needed to bring the organization closer to its long-term goals. These practices inspire and reassure employees so they can try new things and build on each other's ideas.

There are six categories of practice in this quadrant: awareness raising, championing, inviting, experimenting, reenvisioning and sharing.

The quadrant that depicts the formal practices aimed at innovation is called **instilling capacity for change.**

Practices in this quadrant aim to create structures or supports that will form a foundation for future changes in the organization.

There are two categories of practices: learning and developing.

The 59 practices are grouped into categories and distributed across the four quadrants as shown in Figure 10: Framework practices (Bertels, Papania, & Papania, 2010).

It should be noted, at this point, that the use of the term informal does not mean the practices in these quadrants are unstructured or random. In fact, they are quite the opposite. They are structured practices that will leverage informal channels and lead to successful change.

For example, in the quadrant called fostering commitment that contains informal practices for delivering on current commitments, there is a category called manage talent. The practices within this category are recruit people, allocate people and promote people.

These structured practices will result in informal change levers. These include attracting, retaining and motivating staff. Motivated people are willing to disseminate information and coordinate action that contributes to embedding change.

Promotion of supporters of change sends a strong message to other employees indicating the importance of this behavior to the organization. This can drive changes in current behavior toward desired behavior that support the change.

It is these values and behaviors, which have developed informally, that are codified and organized through the formal practices.

A portfolio approach

As already mentioned, organizations should draw practices from all four quadrants of the framework in the effort to embed changes.

Similar to the need to consume food from each of the food groups for good health, it is a balanced approach, and uses a wide and diverse range of practices that will achieve successful organizational change.

Those working to embed change into the organization need a **portfolio** of practices at their disposal. The portfolio of practices creates a balanced diversity to ensure successful change.

The approach can be used for strategic, tactical and operational change. It can be used for small, medium and large changes of varying complexity and priority. It can be used to increase resilience in the face of constant change.

Using the framework

There are a number of ways in which the framework can be used. It can be used to assess a current change initiative and perform a gap analysis or it can be used for planning the approach to future change initiatives. The following two sections explore the use of the framework in each of those contexts.

Current initiatives

The framework can be used to provide a baseline and gap assessment of your current change and improvement initiatives.

Scan across the four quadrants of the framework and determine to what extent you currently make use of a particular practice within each quadrant.

For each practice, determine those you do and don't use.

What you are looking for is a balance across all four quadrants. It doesn't have to be a perfect balance but you want to eliminate heavy use of one quadrant over another.

Of the practices that you don't currently use, identify those you could employ to bring about a balanced approach.

For those practices you currently employ, determine whether to increase or decrease the use of that practice to bring about balance. You may decide to eliminate the use of a practice you currently employ in order to use the resources allocated to that practice elsewhere.

Figure 11 is an example of an unbalanced portfolio.

In this example, there is heavy use of practices in the clarifying expectations quadrant and little use of practices in the instilling capacity for change quadrant.

The emphasis in this example is on formal and informal practices targeted at delivering on current commitments. There is minimal use of practices, both formal and informal, aimed at innovation.

The practices currently being employed to embed a change into the organization need to be revisited so that a balanced approach is obtained. The outcome should be a balanced portfolio as shown in Figure 12.

Future initiatives

The framework can be used to plan new change and improvement initiatives and ensure that there will be a balanced approach.

With a particular change initiative in mind, scan across the four quadrants and select a diversified subset of practices that are best suited to your organization and / or team for implementing and embedding this change into the organization.

Ensure that you select practices from each of the four quadrants.

The key is to have a balance across the framework to give you a portfolio approach. Make sure you are not expending too much energy on the practices in one quadrant at the expense of those in another. Figure 12 is an example of a balanced portfolio.

The number and type of practices you choose will depend on the resources and capabilities you have available to employ those practices. Don't choose more practices than you are capable of employing effectively.

Consideration needs to be given to the capabilities e.g. skills and experience, as well as the resources e.g. people, time, finances etc. that will be needed to effectively employ the chosen practices. This should include use of both internally and externally available capabilities and resources.

The number and type of practices may also be driven by the nature of the change or initiative being planned. For example, a strategic change or initiative that is going to have widespread impact across the entire organization may warrant a larger number of practices than for an operational or tactical change.

An operational change or initiative that is limited to a small group of people may only need one practice from each quadrant of the framework to effectively embed the change.

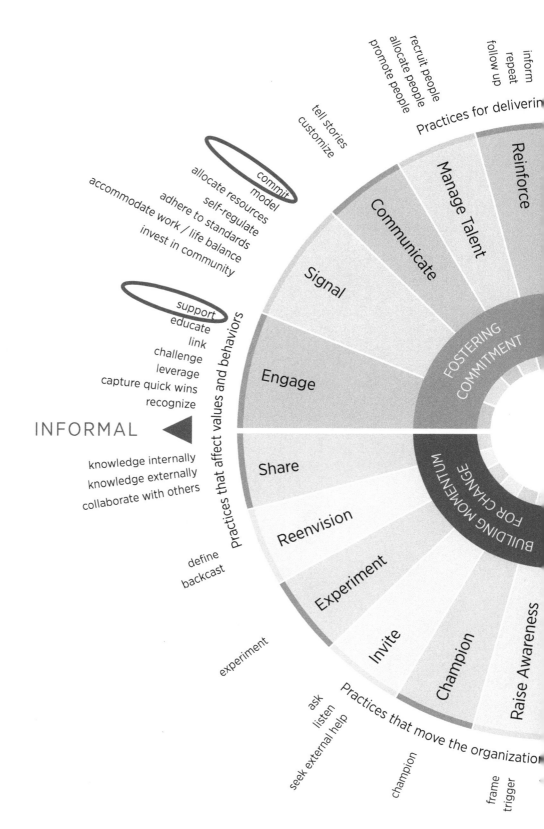

Figure 11: An example of an unbalanced portfolio

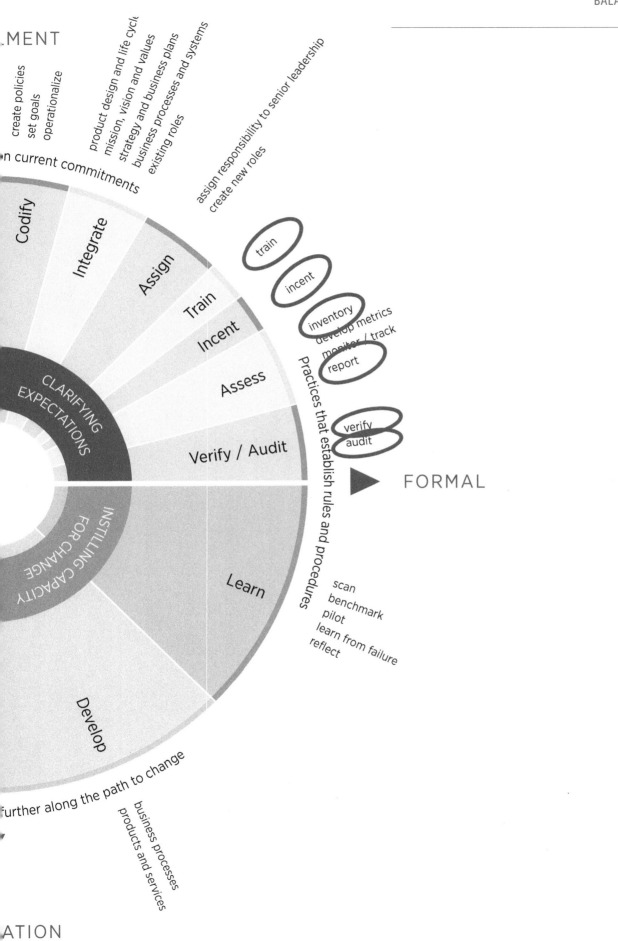

LMENT

create policies
set goals
operationalize

product design and life cycle
mission, vision and values
strategy and business plans
business processes and systems
existing roles

n current commitments

assign responsibility to senior leadership
create new roles

Codify

Integrate

Assign

Train

Incent

Assess

Verify / Audit

CLARIFYING
EXPECTATIONS

INSTILLING
CAPACITY
FOR CHANGE

train

incent

inventory
develop metrics
monitor / track
report

verify
audit

Practices that establish rules and procedures

FORMAL

scan
benchmark
pilot
learn from failure
reflect

Learn

Develop

further along the path to change

business processes
products and services

ATION

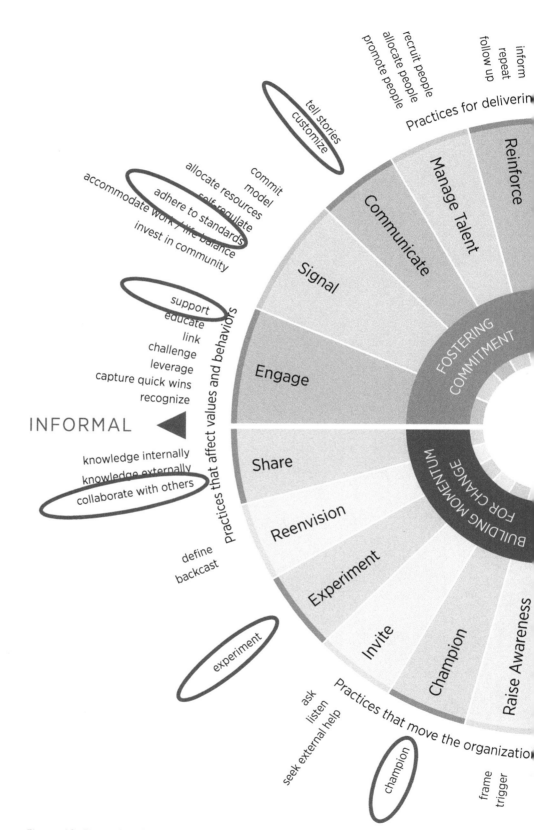

Figure 12: Example of a balanced portfolio

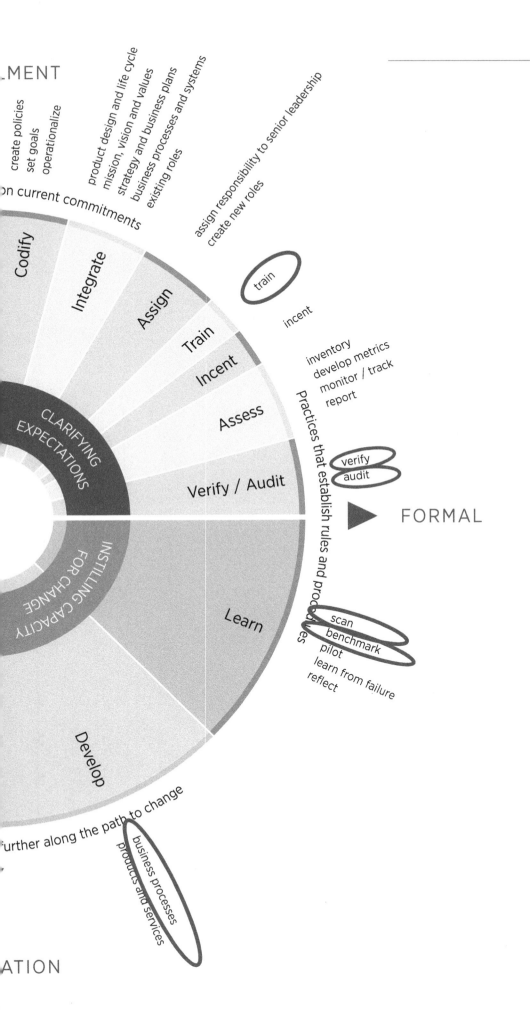

LMENT

create policies
set goals
operationalize

product design and life cycle
mission, vision and values
strategy and business plans
business processes and systems
existing roles

on current commitments

assign responsibility to senior leadership
create new roles

Codify

Integrate

Assign

Train

Incent

Assess

Verify / Audit

CLARIFYING
EXPECTATIONS

INSTILLING
CAPACITY
FOR CHANGE

Learn

Develop

train

incent

inventory
develop metrics
monitor / track
report

verify
audit

Practices that establish rules and procedures

▶ FORMAL

scan
benchmark
pilot
learn from failure
reflect

further along the path to change

business processes
products and services

ATION

Fostering commitment

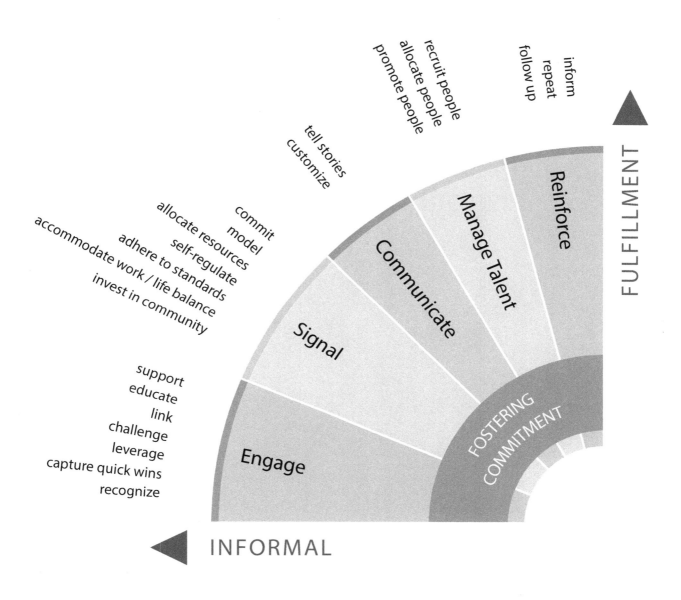

Figure 13: Fostering commitment quadrant

Fostering commitment includes the informal practices aimed at supporting the goal of delivering on existing commitments. These practices aim to motivate employees to get involved, to reinforce the importance of the change for the organization, and to support and encourage those who are already making efforts to embed the change into the organization.

There are five categories and 22 practices.

QUADRANT	CATEGORY	PRACTICES
Fostering commitment	Engage	Support
		Educate
		Link
		Challenge
		Leverage
		Capture quick wins
		Recognize
	Signal	Commit
		Model
		Allocate resources
		Self-regulate
		Adhere to standards
		Accommodate work / life balance
		Invest in the community
	Communicate	Tell stories
		Customize
	Manage Talent	Recruit
		Allocate people
		Promote
	Reinforce	Inform
		Repeat
		Follow up

Table 7: Fostering commitment categories and practices

Engage

This category consists of informal practices that attempt to raise the level of employee engagement throughout the organization. These practices aim to generate interest and excitement among employees about the change journey and to encourage employees to participate actively in initiatives.

These practices help motivate employees to act in a way that brings the organization closer to the goal of the change. The practices that relate to engagement include educating, challenging, linking, supporting, leveraging, capturing quick wins and recognizing.

Research has revealed the benefits of employee engagement[2]:

- Employee engagement results in reduced absenteeism and increased productivity.
- Employee engagement correlates with increased retention.

- Employee engagement leads to increased commitment to quality and safety.
- Employee engagement results in increased profitability.

Support

Make it easier for employees to adopt change(s):

- Provide support for employees to adopt the change.
- Remove barriers.

Support should include access to resources, education, open channels to discuss and ask questions, and regular communication and engagement. There should be regular feedback loops.

Barriers to teamwork and collaboration should be removed. Platforms for effective collaboration should be available across the enterprise.

Barriers to teamwork and collaboration could include:

- Lack of trust and respect
- Poor communication and listening skills
- Organizational silos
- Geographical distribution.

There are many others, but I think these are the four key barriers.

Lack of trust and respect can be overcome by increasing the interactions between teams, departments and / or business units. Establishing an understanding of the roles of other areas, their challenges and the value that they deliver can start to build trust and respect. Increase the channels of two-way communication between different areas. Encourage cross-functional working on shared projects. Leaders should model collaboration and walk the talk.

Poor communication and listening skills can be addressed through educational workshops where employees are not just told what effective communication and listening looks like but where they are able to try them out in a safe environment. This is an environment in which they can try new skills and know it is okay to not get them right the first time. They can keep trying until they master them. Employees should be encouraged to provide real-time feedback and call out poor communication and listening so that it can be addressed.

Organizational silos often exist because there is reluctance to share knowledge and information. Often, there is a lack of alignment with organizational goals and objectives. Different areas of the business need to come together and align their goals and objectives with those of the organization. This results in a shared sense of purpose. Cross-functional working can help break down silos.

Geographical distribution is a challenge but a common one today. There will always be the challenge of time zones, culture, language and religion etc. Employee education in diversity and inclusion may be needed. Technology can remove geographical boundaries to collaboration and should be leveraged to meet needs.

Barriers could also include insufficient communication and engagement, and poor management. The former can be removed through increased effective communication and engagement while the latter should be addressed by the organizational change management professional within the organization who is tasked with setting the change management strategy and ensuring the organization is an adaptive and resilient one in the face of constant change.

If there are managers who are not adaptive to change and who are creating a barrier to change, then this has to be dealt with. They can be educated and coached to become effective leaders and if that does not happen, more drastic action will have to take place.

When an organization is required to constantly change and evolve to remain relevant, there is no place for management that cannot adapt and lead change.

Support for employees adopting a new way of working, whether that be process or technology driven, should be given through early access to playbooks, workshops and sandpits. Provision of safe environments in which employees can try out the new ways of working support early adoption.

Resistance to change is a barrier to be removed through identification of the cause of resistance and making interventions as necessary. When an organization has a focus on building a workforce that is resilient and always commits to communicating the 'why' for change, resistance is lowered if not mitigated.

Organizations should also support employees with the provision of the skills and capabilities to be resilient in the face of constant and uncertain change. Resources, training, education and support need to be available to ensure employee resilience. Leaders need to be competent in the identification of low resilience and know what actions to take.

My 2020 publications *Unleash the Resiliator Within—Resilience: A Handbook for Individuals* and *Unleash the Resiliator Within—Resilience: A handbook for Leaders* addresses these needs.

Educate

Raise the level of awareness and understanding of the change through the provision of information in informal ways:

- Include information about the change(s) and initiative(s) that are underway in organizational newsletters, bulletin boards, posters, websites, social media channels and online forums etc.
- Run 'brown bag' sessions to provide information to the attendees in a voluntary and informal setting.
- Invite employees to hear speakers who are experts in the area that the change(s) or initiative(s) is focused on.

Provide education relating to change(s) and initiative(s) underway through informal channels.

You may consider some of the channels listed here as formal but when people are invited rather than instructed to partake of the education, I am classing that as 'informal'.

Employees have the option to read a newsletter rather than being directed to attend a presentation from the CEO.

Education increases awareness and understanding. Do not forget that all education should address the 'why' of the change or initiative not just the 'what' and 'how'. The 'why' is the most powerful message.

We often focus on the 'what we need to do' and 'how we are going to do it' and forget to explain 'the why'. That is like telling me we are going to London (what) and we will be flying on a Boeing 737 (how). I am not engaged because you have not told me 'why' we are going to London.

If employees can understand the 'why', they are more likely to be aligned with the change. For example, consider these two statements provided in education regarding a change initiative:

"We are going to increase customer satisfaction by reducing delivery times."

"If we don't increase customer satisfaction, customer attrition will continue to decrease, and we will be out of business in six months."

Which of those resonates most in regard to the need for change? The first is 'what' and 'how' whereas the second is 'why' and far more powerful.

Ensure that education is available to all stakeholders whether they are directly or indirectly impacted by the change(s).

Be sure to hone your information to the audience you are targeting and determine how much information you 'push' e.g. direct e-mail, and how much you allow employees to 'pull' e.g. voluntary attendance at information sessions, intranet content etc.

Do not believe that you can overcommunicate. No-one ever left an organization due to too much communication.

Find different, innovative and exciting ways to deliver messages. If you deliver messages using old, tired and boring methods, you are inferring that your change or initiative is tired and boring. The channel or medium used for communication sends an important message.

You could invite speakers into the organization who are experts in the area of the change(s) you are undertaking.

Google do this well. **Talks at Google** is an internal talks series hosted by Google in Mountain View, California. The talks are hosted for Google employees.

The program invites authors, scientists, actors, artists, filmmakers and musicians to discuss their work. Most of the talks are uploaded to a YouTube channel for later viewing and can also be accessed via Google Podcasts.

Forward thinking organizations should take a leaf out of the Google book. Not only do Google record sessions for later viewing by employees, but it also make them available to people outside of the organization.

This demonstrates commitment to a particular change or initiative and investment in the wider community.

See section Invest in community and Communication.

Link

Bring the change(s) and initiative(s) down to the individual level by connecting the impact of everyday actions at work with those outside the workplace (and vice versa), and connect organizational activities to personal activities (and vice versa):

- Encourage employees to bring their personal behaviors (related to the change or initiative) into the workplace e.g. values, beliefs.
- Encourage employees to carry the organizational change message outside the organization e.g. corporate social responsibility, increasing sustainability, easier access to services for those currently disadvantaged.

Making change relate to individuals makes it more concrete. If a link can be made between employee action at work and their behavior outside work, it can reinforce those behaviors.

Let's take a customer service example.

Employees have expectations of service providers they encounter on a daily basis. This could be in the retail or hospitality sector.

If we encourage employees to recognize those expectations and seek to apply them back in the workplace, we can increase the adoption of changes and initiatives related to improved customer service.

If we can also link the changes and initiatives taking place within the workplace to experiences outside the workplace, it can act as reinforcement.

> I worked for a large financial institution that recognized that customer experience when interacting with banking services needed to change. A program of change was being developed. A way in which to get employees to link the changes that would impact them (internally) with the impact on the customer (externally) was to 'manufacture' a situation where the employee became the customer. They were sent out into the 'real world' to experience the customer experience.
>
> Employees were given tasks including going into a branch and getting online banking and share trading facilities established; trying to make an online insurance claim on the morning of a burglary; using telephone banking to enquire about loan facilities etc.
>
> Employees were encouraged to share both the positive and negative aspects of their experiences.
>
> The outcome of these tasks revealed the difficulty that branch staff had due to poor technology, a website that was not intuitive and services that were not designed with the customer in mind.

Assignment of employees into other areas of the organization can also provide links with the need for changes.

For example, sending technology personnel to a warehouse; sending customer service personnel into a retail store; sending design personnel into a hospital reception; sending health and safety personnel onto a construction site; and sending security personnel into a shopping mall.

This allows employees to experience what their colleagues in other parts of the business and the customers experience. This links changes planned or underway to remove the negative experience with the employees encounter.

Placing employees in the shoes of their colleagues and the customer can provide positive linkages between changes and their importance to the organization.

Challenge

Encourage and recognize good ideas or efforts through internal competitions:

- Encourage employees to challenge the status quo.
- Organize competitions relating to change(s) between individuals, teams, departments, business units and geographical locations.
- Use internal competitions to encourage the generation and identification of new ways of doing things.

Encourage and recognize those who challenge the status quo. Reward creativity, experimentation and innovation.

The key to encouraging challenge and innovation is to provide an environment of psychological safety. This is where employees feel they can speak up, challenge the way things are done, ask questions and be curious etc. without fear of being punished or humiliated. This environment, and positive reinforcement of desired behaviors, motivates employees to think outside the box.

In a world where innovation will be the key to organizational success, employees must feel that their ideas will be heard and that they are valued.

Challenge and innovation can be encouraged through gamification. Whereas games are for fun and play, gamification can be used to engage, motivate and inspire.

A great example of gamification for innovation is Quirky.[3]

Quirky encourages its community of inventors to create and submit an idea for a consumer product. The community votes on the ideas they like the best. Quirky then choses the products to move into development. The community again collaborates including choosing a product name and picking a price point.

Quirky uses 'influence' as a points system for collaboration. This means that collaborators providing skills and services receive 'influence' and share a percentage of the product royalties.

Every organization has a vast ensemble of employees with untapped ideas. This ensemble can be encouraged to share these ideas, collaborate with others and be directed toward creating innovative products, processes and services through gamification.

Organizations can use various gamification techniques to encourage innovation and the adoption of change. These techniques include (but are not limited to):

- Points earned for submitting ideas or for having ideas accepted.
- Points earned for adopting new ways of working.
- Shared virtual currency for the most innovative teams.
- Competitions for submitting the best solution or idea to a specified problem or challenge.
- Leader boards that show the most active employees and / or the most active teams.
- Leader boards that show the most successful employees and / or the most successful teams.

It is vital to ensure that any competition is a positive experience and does not alienate employees. Competition should drive desired behaviors not unfavorable ones.

Here is an example of competition at a software development company that drove the wrong behaviors.

The company wanted to encourage the testing team to work harder at finding errors and bugs. It decided to award virtual currency for every bug that the testing team could find. Then, to drive the elimination of the bugs, it awarded the development team the same currency for the bugs that were fixed.

The result was a black market in bugs. The developers would only get currency if they made bugs and the testers found them. In essence, they were getting paid to create bugs.

Developers would intentionally write simple and obvious bugs and then turn them over to the testers with information to the whereabouts of the bug. The testers would quickly hand the code back, having detected the bug, and the developers would instantly fix it.

Within a short period, all productive work had ceased. The organization just created bugs, identified them and fixed them for a couple of days until the error of the incentive was recognized.

In this example, it was not only the award to the individual that drove undesired behavior but also the fact that if the developers had worked hard to avoid bugs, they would have made it hard for the testers to get any rewards for detecting the bugs. It also meant that the behavior of one team was to the detriment of another.

Competition and gamification can be powerful tools but each needs to be designed carefully in order to have the desired results.

Gamification in relation to change(s) could follow this pattern:

Round one

Situation: Employees do not know why their current way of working needs to change.

Action: Raising awareness and recognition of the need for change.

Round two

Situation: Employees do not understand the value in changing ways for working.

Action: Getting buy-in and commitment to the change.

Round three

Situation: Employees do not know how to change ways of working. They lack the knowledge.

Action: Education in regard to changing ways of working.

Round four

Situation: Employees are still coming to terms with the adoption of the new ways of working.

Action: In addition to the knowledge provided in round three, provide the ability to adopt new ways of working through testing and experimentation.

Round five

Situation: Employees understand what is needed but the change is not yet embedded into business-as-usual activity.

Action: Reinforcement of the need for change. This could be through celebration of successes, continued education, rewards and recognition, and continual feedback loops.

Leverage

Encourage and support grassroots efforts; try to amplify the effect of activities initiated by individuals or small groups:

- Provide company time to meet about conceiving and launching initiatives related to the change.
- Provide time and resources to support ideas initiated by employees.

Leveraging is a way to encourage employees to adopt and drive change. Grassroots efforts to change to new ways of working should be encouraged and recognized.

Successful change is more often than not driven from the grassroots up rather than from the mountain top down.

Provide employees with a way in which they can raise their ideas and then have discussions, brainstorming sessions and debates around them. This could be an idea portal on the intranet that allows employees to lodge and share their ideas, which can then be discussed and voted on.

Ensure everyone knows that no idea is a bad idea. It may not get off the ground, but all ideas are valued contributions.

Some examples of organizations leveraging employee ideas include Toyota.

"Never be satisfied with what you have got" is a core Toyota principle. Every employee is expected to come up with ideas for improvement each month. This includes everyone from the front line to the CEO.

They are also provided with the time and resources to do so.

The concept of 'Kaizen' used at Toyota, refers to activities that continually improve all functions and come from all employees. Continual improvement is a part of every employee's job description.

Google is another example. Google encourages employees to devote 20% of their time to innovation and change. Not all employees take advantage of this '20 % policy' due to competing demands but the principle is still in place. The story goes that the '20% time' policy resulted in the creation of Gmail.

Organizations have to provide the time and space for innovation and change. When engineers at Intel complained that they did not have enough time and space to be creative, the company piloted 'thinking time'. Each Tuesday morning, employees were encouraged to take their work offline. This meant canceling meetings, call forwarding to voicemail, and out-of-office messages on e-mail.

This might sound radical but unless time, space and isolation from distractions can be provided, change and innovation may be stifled.

Atlassian prides itself on its culture of innovation and provides time and space to let its employees' creative and innovative juices flow. It recognizes that the innovation culture will vary throughout offices as the organization is spread over several continents. Teams across Atlassian practice different forms of structured innovation, for example, '20% time' one day a week, 'Innovation Week', which takes place one week out of five and games from the team playbook such as 'Disrupt' and 'Sparring.' Whatever form is adopted, teams are given space and dedicated time for creative thinking.

Changes driven from the bottom up are far more likely to succeed than the ones driven from the top down.

Capture quick wins

Identify and complete changes related to the initiative that are less demanding of resources or that result in readily identifiable benefits (also called 'low hanging fruit').

- Start with the low hanging fruit.

Identifying quick wins is a means to build momentum for the change(s) within the organization. Small successes can be used to overcome areas of resistance.

However, once the quick wins are exhausted, a more structured plan for moving forward will need to be developed.

Quick wins are an important tactic for demonstrating that the new approach is effective in order to encourage already enthusiastic supporters to get behind future change programs.

Quick wins are important because they:

- Prove a point. The point being that the change can happen (and change can work).
- Provide the change with credibility.
- Creative momentum. A change that is to take place over a long period of time, without any visibility of progress, will not be sustainable. Employees will not be motivated and ready for adoption. Complacency will set in. Quick win after quick win maintains the momentum and motivation for change.
- Allow storytelling. Effective communication is key and using the power of storytelling to describe quick wins can get employee buy-in to change. Stories can help employees to visualize a change in action, see the results the change brings, and get excited about those results.
- Provide a cause for celebration. Celebration of quick wins builds resilience and the willingness to keep changing. It provides organizational-wide visibility of the change if undertaken and announced publicly.

Quick wins have to be designed and led by those leading change. You cannot expect them to just happen albeit sometimes you might get an unexpected surprise.

It is important to ensure quick wins are planned, scheduled and that the required resources to develop and implement them are allocated. It is also important to communicate the implementation and results of quick wins to all stakeholders.

Recognize

Show awareness and approval or appreciation of efforts to adopt the change(s) through informal accolades:

- Publicly recognize employees at staff meetings.
- Create change awards.
- Hold celebrations.

Unlike the formal practice of incentives where compensation is directly tied to specific measures or outcomes, recognition involves informal attempts to indicate approval or appreciation for efforts related to the organizational change(s).

Create awards as well as celebrating change successes. Adopt a democratic approach e.g. staff nominations of peers for rewards.

Ensure that rewards are given for efforts that are above and beyond what is expected from individuals in their day-to-day work.

Make sure that awards and recognitions do not become devalued through overuse or misuse.

Do not overstructure this informal practice so that it loses meaning. For example, implementing monthly team awards where an award has to be made every month. This results in awards being allocated based on a necessity to fulfil a monthly obligation rather than on merit.

Recognition of desired behaviors is often called positive reinforcement. Positive reinforcement directly rewards the behavior you want to see in your employees. Clearly, this means that you need to know the behaviors you want to see more of and the behaviors you want to see less of.

The key to positive reinforcement is clarity regarding what is being recognized and the timing.

Recognition and positive reinforcement should happen while the employee is doing the job. It should be done in a timely manner where it is clear what is being recognized. The employee and / or the team should be left in no doubt as to what has generated the recognition.

The longer the time between the behavior and the recognition / reinforcement, the less effective it is. This is exactly why annual performance reviews have little or no impact on behavior.

Effective recognition and reinforcement means that you have to know the recipient(s). What mix of recognition and reinforcement will work best?

Everyone is different and, therefore, will respond differently. What interests and motivates them? What is important to them?

It can take time to find this information, but it is simply acquired through conversation, listening and engagement.

What are their motivators? What gives them the most satisfaction? What areas can be targeted as those to be recognized and reinforced?

Recognition and reinforcements could include (but are not limited to):

- Highlighting accomplishments
- Public recognition and praise
- Saying thank-you
- Gift cards
- Concert or movie tickets
- Celebration breakfast / lunch / dinner
- Drinks after work
- Career progression
- Monetary rewards
- A pat on the back.

It is important to note that when you accept, tolerate or permit unacceptable behaviors i.e. those you don't wish to see, you are rewarding those employees as well by allowing them to continue with that behavior with no consequences.

Signal

This category consists of practices that serve to identify the change(s) as a priority for the organization. An organization's actions send strong messages regarding its position on the change(s) to its employees.

This category of practices includes actions or gestures that serve to communicate the importance of the change(s) to employees in informal ways.

These practices include committing publicly, modeling, allocating resources, self-regulating, adhering, accommodating, work / life balance and investing in the community.

Commit

- Have the organization and / or senior leadership make a public commitment to the change(s).
- Make commitments to the change(s) public.
- Whenever possible, include messages about the change(s) in company presentations and media releases.
- Include metrics and targets related to the change(s) in company publications such as annual reports and CxO reports.

One way to signal commitment to change is for the organizational leadership teams to speak openly about company goals and the progress toward them.

Leadership teams can show commitment to the change(s) by writing a letter to employees stating their commitment clearly and concisely with no room for ambiguity.

They can create a video in which they talk about commitment to change, which can be made available internally and externally.

They can talk about the change(s) in leadership and management forums internally and externally.

They can discuss change(s) in informal settings such as town halls or brown-bag lunches. They can engage on collaboration channels to take and answer questions about the change(s) thus demonstrating commitment.

Talking about the change(s) outside the organization is powerful. Committing publicly to change(s) can serve as a powerful motivator for employees.

Remember that a message delivered externally may have a stronger impact on employees than a message delivered only internally.

There are various ways in which leaders can demonstrate their commitment to change.

In their book *The Practice of Adaptive Leadership*, Ronald Heifetz and Marty Linksy use the analogy of the balcony and the dance floor. They describe a leader's ability to perceive, observe and intervene as moving between the dance floor and the balcony.

When on the dance floor, the observation is different from when on the balcony. When you are dancing, you are focusing on the music. Your impression is that everyone is having a great time.

When you retreat to the balcony and watch over the dance floor, you may observe that some people are not dancing at all and that there appears to be a departure of people from the dance floor when the music speeds up or gets louder.

You could not make these observations while on the dance floor. Now you have a clearer picture of what is happening and you have gained some perspective.

On the balcony, you do your observing of patterns, reflecting, option thinking, analyzing and monitoring of change(s).

When leaders what to intervene, they have to get back on the dance floor and operate in the fray as opposed to above it.

Adaptive leaders show their commitment to change by operating both on the balcony and on the dance floor. They get out from behind the desk and walk around the organization and meet people in their places of work. They get to know their employees and they truly listen to what they have to say. They then get back on the balcony (behind the desk) and make things happen. They address what they have heard. This demonstrates commitment to change(s).

Leaders can also demonstrate commitment by walking the talk. They ensure that their own behavior and language support the change(s).

They make sure that employees have the resources they need. They remove barriers, keep the momentum going and see it through to the end.

They hold themselves accountable and deliver on their promises in relation to the change(s).

Model

Enact the roles and behaviors organizational leaders wish employees to emulate:

- Demonstrate leadership by 'walking the walk' and 'talking the talk'.
- Participate in ongoing discussions about the change journey.
- Prioritize the change(s) in discussions and decision-making.
- Back up colleagues and employees when they prioritize the change(s).
- Show interest in the work of those involved in making the change(s).

The commitment of leadership is a critical success factor for embedding change. It is imperative that leaders signal their support for the change. This can be achieved through role modeling.

Employees are far more likely to try out new behaviors if they see them modeled by others whom they respect and admire.

Leaders modeling new behaviors in support of the change(s) gives credibility to the goals being pursued throughout the organization. Leadership can signal commitment by 'practicing what they preach' including prioritizing the change(s) in their decision-making.

Another way to send a strong signal is to support employees when they make a decision to prioritize the change(s). Leaders need to show an interest in the work of those involved in the change(s) and participate in the ongoing dialogue in relation to the change(s).

Leaders can also look for opportunities to reinforce positive steps that employees are taking to support the change(s).

Throughout change, leaders must demonstrate integrity and act consistently with what they're asking of their employees.

They need to:

- Express the desired behaviors.
- Model the desired behaviors.
- Reward the desired behaviors through recognition and positive reinforcement.
- Be consistent.

A key requirement for leaders to effectively model change is to be aligned. There needs to be consistency of messages regardless of which leader you are listening to. If there are mixed messages, then employees will not buy in to the change.

Leaders modeling change have a number of behaviors they all share:

- They have a shared purpose. Their narrative is compelling. They answer the question 'why', which is far more important and powerful than the 'what' and 'how'. They also discuss, 'why not?' If leaders cannot articulate a clear message behind the change(s) being made, employees will not get on board.
- They talk about change as a constant and are always looking to the future. They talk about the need to look ahead and seize opportunities or resolve problems before anyone else does.

- They provide time, space and resources for experimentation, creativity and innovation. They cannot promote the need for the organization to constantly evolve and change if they don't back that up with action.
- They work with other leaders and model the need for cross-functional collaboration while establishing an environment of mutual trust and respect.
- They create an environment of psychological safety in which employees feel safe to ask questions about change(s), challenge decision-making, and speak up with ideas, queries or concerns. Leaders model this behavior by asking for feedback, acknowledging their mistakes, being open to opinions different from theirs and encouraging employees to question and challenge without any fear of reprimand. When employees speak up, they are positively acknowledged for doing so.

Allocate resources

Back up the commitment to the change(s) with an allocation of time, money and people:

- Provide time to participate in change activities.
- Allocate employees to execute change initiatives.
- Provide financial resources for change(s).

Another way to signal the importance of the change is to allocate resources. Allocating time and money to an issue helps place it on the organization's strategic agenda. It also acts as a signal to stress the importance of the change(s) to the organization.

Employees should be provided with time and resources that they can apply to creative problem-solving at their discretion.

Leaders needs to allocate resources to the change(s) and communicate that they are willing to do so.

Commitment to change is demonstrated by committing extensive resources in the form of finance, leadership, assigned employees, high quality training, time, skills and capabilities, and collaboration and engagement tools.

If change(s) cannot be adequately resourced, it sends a message that the change(s) is not important. If the change is a priority for the organization, then capable resources need to be assigned to it. It also has to be recognized that these resources are now working on change(s) and not business-as-usual activities. Leaders and employees have to agree the allocation of time to change(s) and time to business as usual. This then has to be honored. Once again, if allocation is just lip service, it sends the wrong messages about the change(s).

The resources allocated to change(s) need to have the skills and competencies to be able to contribute effectively. If resources without these requirements are allocated, it is not only devastating for the employee who has been hung out to dry, but also sends the message that the change is not important.

For example, what if you told your family that building an extra bedroom, of the highest quality, for Grandma was an absolute priority and that you were committed to delivering on that promise. You then allocate tradespeople whom you know do not have the required skills and competencies to carry out the work. You don't allocate the agreed budget and instead use the cheapest resources available.

What message do your actions send? They says, "I am not committed to this change nor do I see it as a priority."

Self-regulate

Implement voluntary initiatives. Adopt best practices in the absence of, or in advance of, regulation:

- Adopt voluntary codes of practice developed internally or at the industry level.
- Adopt best practice frameworks.

Self-regulating is about making choices; it is about being willing to place constraints on how the organization operates in order to make faster progress toward a desired future.

Codes of practice themselves establish new norms. While they often lack strong external sanctions for noncompliance, the potential for transformation rests in the potential for peer pressure both internal to the organization and from industry peers who have also adopted voluntary codes of practice.

A code of practice defines organizational goals, values and principles, and provides every employee with expectations of their behavior.

Organizational change should not be carried out without reference to the code of practice to ensure that the change is in keeping with it and its intent.

Self-regulation, whether against an internal code of practice or an external best practice framework, ensures that change(s) are aligned with organizational purpose and aspiration.

Voluntary codes of practice are codes of practice that influence, shape, control or set benchmarks for organizational behavior. They encourage the organization to conduct itself in ways that benefit itself and the community. Voluntary codes of practice can also serve as an indicator to customers that the organization's product, service or activity meets certain standards.

The following are two examples of voluntary codes of practice to which every change within participating organizations will have to be assessed. Recognition that there are codes of practice that guide all change and encourage the right behaviors and activities can increase change adoption.

Consumers International is a nonprofit foundation linking the activities of some 200 consumer groups in over 80 countries and has developed a Consumer Charter for Global Business. The charter obliges participating companies to meet standards pertaining to ethical conduct (e.g. bribery), competitiveness, marketing practices, guarantees and complaints handling. Companies wishing to adhere to the charter are subject to an initial investigation by Consumers International.

The World Health Organization Global Code of Practice on the International Recruitment of Health Personnel aims to establish and promote voluntary principles and practices for the ethical international recruitment of health personnel and to facilitate the strengthening of health systems. Member states should discourage active recruitment of health personnel from developing countries facing critical shortages of health workers. The code was designed by member states to serve as a continuous and dynamic framework for global dialogue and cooperation.

Best practice frameworks are reusable practices of organizations that have been shown to be successful in their respective functions. A best practice is a method or technique that has been generally accepted as superior to any alternatives as it produces results that are superior to those achieved by other means, or because it has become a standard way of doing things.

The following are examples of best practice frameworks that provide a level of assurance that changes, where appropriate, are leveraging proven approaches:

- The Chronic Illness Alliance's 'Best Practice Framework' covers all aspects of managing a chronic illness peer support program.
- Capture the Fracture is a best practice framework and global campaign to break the fragility fracture cycle.
- ITIL is a widely accepted best practice approach to IT service management (ITSM).
- Process Classification Framework (PCF).
- Supply Chain Operation Reference (SCOR) model.
- Value Reference Mode (VRM).

Adhere to standards

Comply with a recognized set of standards related to the change(s):

- Gain certification from external agencies e.g. International Organization for Standardization (ISO), Standards Australia, American National Standards Institute (ANSI), Institute of Electrical and Electronics Engineers (IEEE) etc.

Many organizations seeking to embed a particular type of change will choose to make investments in the achievement of certification to specific standards.

Adhering to external standards will signal both internally and externally the organization's commitment to the change(s) and a program of continual quality improvement.

The standards chosen will be dependent on the industry in which the organization resides and the change that the organization is wishing to make.

For example, the following are international industry standards from the ISO to which an organization may wish to comply through the implementation of one or more changes:

- ISO 9000 – Quality Management
- ISO / IEC 27000 – Information Security Management Systems
- ISO 14000 – Environmental Management
- ISO 31000 – Risk Management
- ISO 50001 – Energy Management
- ISO 26000 – Social Responsibility
- ISO 28000 – Specifications for Security Management Systems for the Supply Chain
- ISO 45001 – Occupational Health and Safety
- ISO 22000 – Food Management Systems
- ISO 37001 – Anti-Bribery Management Systems

Accommodate work / life balance

Make an effort to address family / life commitments and social benefits for employees and try to see an employee as a whole person and part of a community external to the organization:

- Provide social benefits for employees.
- Support job flexibility.
- Support the personal growth of employees.

Providing a work / life balance for employees demonstrates the organization's commitment to balancing the demands of the workplace (especially during times of change) with home life.

Work / life balance is the point along a continuum where the demands of our work, personal and professional lives converge. The balance is the time allocated to work, and the time allocated to enjoying yourself and spending time with friends and family.

Change initiatives can bring additional stresses and pressures to employees above and beyond those associated with conducting business as usual. There is the risk of burnout if this is not recognized and accommodated.

Change involves changes to ways of working. Change affects both the organization and the individual. For the latter, change can bring about increases in demands, concerns and uncertainty.

The line between work and personal life has become increasingly blurred as we are all able to be switched on and connected 24/7. Therefore, change can have an effect on employee work / life balance.

Demonstrated commitment to maintaining a healthy work / life balance across the organization will increase employee commitment to change.

Change has to be effectively managed to promote commitment to it. If we wish to increase employee commitment to change, we have to decrease negative impacts on work / life balance.

Leaders of change need to ensure that employees are made aware of the reason for change, (the 'why'), the impact it will have on the organization and the individuals within it, and importantly, the resources available to everyone to help them transition through the change without adverse impact on mind and body.

It is important that concerted efforts are made to ensure that employees see changes as beneficial and will, therefore, support it. This in turn decreases concerns, stress and anxiety and contributes to a healthy work / life balance.

Work / life balance can mean different things to people so there is no one-size-fits-all approach.

This is particularly the case in 2020 and beyond, as most organizations will have to accommodate five generations of employees with a range of differing needs.

As a starting point, organizations should look at creating a flexible work environment as this meets the needs of most employees. A flexible work environment means that employees can choose their own hours of working and work from home if they wish. This flexibility reduces stress, increases job satisfaction and increases resilience.

The ability to work remotely will be key as it allows employees to have more control over their working life.

Organizations may consider the provision of increased amenities to improve employee work / life balance e.g. gyms, day-care assistance, on-site crèches, health-care amenities, relaxation sanctuaries and quiet rooms.

Key to accommodating work / life balance is to ask employees what they need.

Invest in community

Contribute to the community and encourage and enable employees to do the same:

- Encourage employees to take time off to attend special interest groups, local interest groups etc.
- Encourage employees to take time off to help organize industry related events.
- Support industry and community bodies.

Organizations can build commitment to change(s) by demonstrating investment in the community or industry.

Supporting industry or community bodies (related to the area of change) through allocation of resources or allowing employees to take time off to be involved sends a clear message of commitment.

Rather than focusing on the cost and time away from the office, organizations and their leaders should focus on the benefits and demonstrate their commitment to change.

There are lots of benefits to employees attending webinars, seminars, conferences and other industry events relevant to their current or future role. These events will be a mix of physical and virtual events. These events provide networking opportunities where your employees can find out what others are doing and bring back valuable information into the organization.

Employees have a learning opportunity and can garner new skills, find out about best practices and learn from industry experts. They offer a unique learning environment that is hard to duplicate. This learning, when applied back in the organization, could be the catalyst for success of change planned or underway.

Attendance at industry events gives employees a chance to get away from their day-to-day work and experience something new, fresh and exciting.

An event that is high energy can invigorate employees or return to the workplace with more energy, motivation and inspiration.

Communicate

This category consists of informal practices that rely on the ability to communicate both the value of the change(s) and the changing priorities and expectations for how work gets done.

There are two core practices related to communicating: storytelling and customizing.

Storytelling makes use of relatable anecdotes and examples to convey concepts related to the change(s).

Customizing refers to attempts to tailor the organization's message to ensure that it is authentic and relevant for different internal and external audiences.

Effective communication keeps everyone informed about what is happening. When people feel engaged and involved with what is happening around them, they are far more likely to adopt change than they would be if they felt they were being kept in the dark.

So many organizations under communicate fearing they will disengage employees. There is no such thing as overcommunication. No-one ever left an organization due to too much communication.

Here are some tips and tricks for effective communication:

Clarity

There should be clarity of message. The communication and its message should be easily understood. There is no room for ambiguity. If a message is not clear, people will fill in the perceived gaps with their own interpretation. Messages become corrupted but also become the new, but flawed, reality.

Validation

Communication should be validated to ensure the message has been heard as intended. If it has not, take action to address it.

Listen

Often we communicate to respond. We should communicate to listen and then respond. We need to listen to questions people are asking about change(s) and ensure that future communication addresses those questions.

Two-way channel

Communication is not about sending out a blanket e-mail. That is a broadcast. Effective communication takes place when recipients are provided with a channel to ask questions and seek clarification.

Share

When people are asking questions, there are likely to be many others with the same questions who are not prepared to speak up.

Capture questions asked and turn them into Frequently Asked Questions (FAQs) that everyone can access easily.

Medium

Give careful consideration to the medium used for communication. Communication could be verbal or written and could be delivered physically or digitally. The medium will depend on the preference of the receiver(s).

Mediums include face-to-face, over the phone, video conference, e-mail, and text and social media.

Frequency

Consider the frequency of communication of a particular message required by the receiver. While there is no such thing as overcommunication, the frequency of communication should be agreed with the recipients and adjusted as required.

Timing

Timing is important. Consider the best time for the recipients to read and digest the communication. For example, it's probably not an optimum time to run a town hall meeting on a Friday afternoon when most employees are thinking about the weekend. Sending an e-mail first thing on a Monday morning is not an optimum time as it can get lost in the already busy in-boxes filled with weekend mail.

Push or pull?

Communication can be delivered through push or pull methods or both. Again, this should be determined by the needs of the intended audience.

Push methods are where the message is pushed out to the audience; whereas, pull methods are where the audience retrieves the message when they want it. Push methods include e-mail, letter, desk drop, presentations etc.

Pull methods include information hosted on an intranet, a knowledge base or collaboration platform that people can access when and if they wish.

Pictures

It is not a cliché when we say, "a picture paints a thousand words." It is true. For example, which of these is easier to understand?

A circle is a simple closed shape. It is the set of all points in a plan that are at a given distance from a given point, the centre; equivalently, it is the cured traced out by a point that moves so that its distance from a given point is constant.

OR

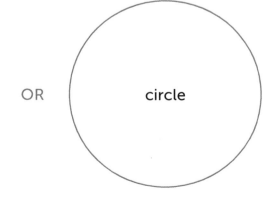

If you can use images and graphics to enhance your message, do so.

Testing

Before delivering communication (verbal or nonverbal), get someone else to read it or listen to it, and ensure it is clear and without ambiguity.

Perform an A/B test when communicating to a wide audience. Use a medium, for example e-mail, where you want the recipients to take a particular course of action such as clicking on a link to access further information. Create two versions of the communication: A and B. Both are intended for the recipient to click on a link within the e-mail.

Version A will have one variable different to Version B. For example, A may contain a graphic and B does not; A may have a different title to B; A may utilize a different font to B.

Send version A to a sample group of 30 people and send version B to another sample group of 30 people. Determine whether communication A or B worked best based on how many people clicked on the link. Use the best performing communication to go to the wider audience.

Communication plan

It is useful to create a communication plan that identifies the audience / stakeholders, the message, the medium to be used, the frequency and timing of the communication, response required, and who is responsible for the communication.

Who (Audience)	What (Message)	Where (Medium)	When (Frequency)	Why (Objective)	How (Responsible)
Change sponsor	Progress report	E-mail	Weekly	Provide progress and raise issues	Change lead
Executive	Progress report (summary)	E-mail	Monthly	Provide summary and raise issues	Change sponsor
Employees (impacted)	Status report	Video comms	Weekly	Inform staff of progress and next steps. Q&A.	Change lead
Employees (interested)	Awareness of change	Bulletin	Monthly	Overview	Change lead

Figure 14: Example of a communication plan

Tell stories

Convey desired behaviors through the use of examples and stories:

- Discuss case studies of successful change initiatives in the organization.
- Create stories about what the organization could look like in the future as a result of change(s).
- Create simple stories and repeat them often, using different means.
- Start every meeting with a quick story related to successful change.
- Use metaphors and symbols.

Storytelling is a highly effective communication method. Stories are illustrative, easily remembered and allow the communicator to create stronger emotional bonds with the recipients.

When we hear stories, we are more engaged than we would be by just hearing about data and facts. When we read or hear data alone, the language part of the brain works to understand it.

When we read or hear a story, parts of the brain that we would use if we were actually experiencing what we are reading or hearing, start working too.

It is far easier to remember stories than data or facts.

Storytelling can open up lines of communication, create integration opportunities and develop a commitment to new values.

Sharing stories of successful changes and lessons learned along the way can support the current change initiative.

Painting a picture of what the future could look like as a result of the change can encourage and inspire people to adopt change.

Ella Saltmarche says that stories have three qualities and narratives that all industry sectors can use to drive change: light, glue and web.[4]

Stories as light help illuminate the past, present and future and, therefore, light up the path of change(s). It describes current issues, those already trying to make a change happen and provide a compelling vision for the future.

Stories as glue is a tool for building community through empathy and coherence. It enables people to connect across difference and to generate narratives that hold together groups, organizations and movements. Empathy allows us to understand what it must feel like to be someone else. Story is a key cohering role in building the groups and movements so essential for change. It helps disparate people from communities.

Stories as web is used to rewrite the web of narratives we live in. It can be used to change the personal narratives we have about our lives, the cultural narratives that frame the issue we advocate for, and change the mythic narratives that influence our world view. Working with myth is integral to the work of changing the values, mindsets, rules and goals of an organization.

Customize

Make or alter to individual or group specifications:

- Translate and adjust the message for different groups.
- Adjust your message for delivery in different types of media.
- Transform the message by adjusting terminology for different operational divisions and levels.

Customization is about taking the key messages related to the change(s) and making them more relevant for the intended audience. Different groups and individuals within the organization may be more receptive to different styles and means of communication.

Avoid a one-size-fits-all approach to communicating change. During change, it is particularly important to customize and target messages to meet the needs of the different employee groups within your organization.

The message needs to be tailored to use terminology that is familiar to a particular audience. Part of the process of embedding change is translating abstract concepts into language that enables employees to understand their application in day-to-day business.

Effective customization of the message depends on knowing your audience, knowing what it cares about and knowing what it wants to hear.

Getting to know the various stakeholder groups and how you need to customize your messages about change can take some time but as a rule of thumb you can ask yourself, or others, the following questions:

- What are their challenges and needs?
- What is top of their mind at the moment?
- What are their concerns?

In your communication, addressing these questions shows that you care and it gets the recipient's attention.

Then try and answer the question in regard to the change: "Why should they care?" If you can answer this question, you have made a connection.

Manage talent

The practices in this category describe how staffing decisions support the transition toward the achievement of the change(s). Managing talent involves hiring people with the passion, attitude and competence to make the changes(s) happen and placing the right people in the right roles across the organization.

Managing talent is about engaging the right people, having the right people in the right roles and recognizing performance. Employee engagement and retention of talent is a key driver in this area.

The practices include recruiting, allocating and promoting.

Recruit people

Identify and hire people with the required orientation and skills:

- Refer to the change initiatives that are planned and underway in recruiting materials.
- Integrate the goals and values of the organization and change initiatives into all job advertisements.
- Make sure the required orientation and skills are clearly specified in the job advertisements.
- Make quality improvement through change a part of all job descriptions for new hires.
- Select new employees on a basis of commitment to quality improvement through change.
- Attempt to foster productive diversity through hiring decisions.

To build and support a culture of change and quality improvement, an organization's recruiting and selection processes should strategically build a pool of human capital with values and skills that support the change journey.

Organizations with a strong reputation for continual quality improvement will attract employees who want to work in a changing environment.

Seek candidates who can provide practical examples of leading and / or driving change within an organization and explore the challenges they faced and how they overcame them.

A good interview approach is the STAR technique (situation, task, approach and result). Although this is often used as a technique for the interviewee, it is also a useful tool for the interviewer to determine whether the candidate has real experience in the area of interest.

SITUATION: Ask the candidate to describe the situation in which they found themselves due to change, whether they were impacted, leading or driving change.

TASK: Ask the candidate to describe the task that faced them to rectify or improve the situation.

APPROACH: The candidate should be able to describe in detail the approach they took as well as any problems they had to overcome.

RESULT: The result of the actions should be described and explored and whether the desired outcome was achieved.

It is also useful to ask whether the candidate would have done anything different if faced with the same situation again. This will indicate whether the candidate has captured lessons learned from the situation to improve future approaches to change.

Include the need for continual change for organizational success as part of all job descriptions. This could include the need for all employees to contribute actively to a program of change through submission of ideas for improvement, membership of working groups to identify improvements and active participation in change initiatives.

It is also good to foster a team of diverse individuals. Ideally, they should all have a shared set of values and beliefs but there should be a spread of personalities, backgrounds and experiences.

A team consisting wholly of 'blue-sky' thinkers will struggle to come up with improvement ideas that have some grounding in reality.

A team consisting wholly of cautious people will prevent the team from thinking outside of the square.

When you have a diverse team, you are bringing in different experiences, knowledge and talent. The team is working toward a common goal using different skill sets.

Allocate people

Move the people who are passionate about the area of change(s) into roles associated with those change(s):

* Identify people with a passion for the area of change and place them in key roles.
* Identify people with the related skills and technical knowledge and place them where their skills are needed.

An important aspect of staffing is ensuring that the talent you already have gets allocated to the right positions within the organization. In particular, key roles must be staffed by people with appropriate training who are dedicated to the area of change.

Selecting the right people is key to moving toward a culture of continual improvement through change.

Choosing cooperative, motivated people to work as a steering group or as change advocates, while simultaneously excluding those who are against or ambivalent to the change, is critical to developing strategies that move the organization toward quality improvement.

This is a behavior that is not exhibited by many organizations. It is the brave organization that is prepared to act in this way in the interest of successful change.

In sports, when you are selecting a winning team, you don't select players who are not interested in playing and winning the game. Those players will sit on the bench until they change or they will leave the team.

The same applies to managing change in organizations. You select the team that is going to win.

Motivated people are willing to disseminate information and coordinate action that contributes to the embedding of quality improvement.

This is not to say that work should not be done to change the position of the dissenter to one of advocate. When this happens, it sends a powerful message to employees.

Promote people

Move people with the right values and skills into higher positions within the organization:

- Make performance, in relation to change(s), a criterion in promotion decisions.
- Reward employees demonstrating a commitment to change(s).
- Include principles and goals, in relation to change(s), in promotion criteria.

Recognizing employee commitment and dedication to the goals of a change through promotion not only places the best people in those roles but also sends a powerful message to other employees indicating the importance of this behavior to the organization.

Embed commitment and active support of constant change into performance management systems. Note that I do not mean the once-a-year performance appraisal as an effective performance management system. Performance management systems should comprise regular check-ins and frequent (real-time) feedback.

These regular check-ins are discussions that focus on the development of employees. They allow the employee to discuss what has worked well and how that success can be repeated in the future. It allows them to explore the challenges they faced and how they could be overcome moving forward. Actions are agreed (by both parties) to develop the employee and further improve their performance.

Reinforce

The practices in this category emphasize the importance of the change(s).

Organizations must constantly reinforce the message in various ways to embed it in the hearts and minds of all employees. Without reinforcement, there may be a preference to revert to the 'old ways' of working and the change will not deliver the desired results.

Regular checkpoints and reviews should be performed to keep the change(s) on the organizational agenda and to maintain momentum.

The practices include informing, repeating and following up.

Inform

Act repeatedly to keep employees informed, appraised and up to date:

- Communicate change progress widely across the organization.
- Keep employees up to date on the organization's current change activities and future plans.

Organizations should communicate regular updates on their current initiatives and future endeavors to all employees.

If employees are not familiar with current change programs and the intended future direction, they may feel excluded or detached from the organization and its ambitions. They will become disengaged.

Good communication from the top of the organization—and back up—is important. There needs to be open channels of communication so that employees can ask questions and raise concerns. Questions, which are asked on a regular basis, should form a set of frequently asked questions (FAQ's) that are made available and easily accessible to employees.

Various methods of communication can be utilized to keep employees informed and up to date. These can include scorecards, portals, bulletin boards, newsletters, team meetings, one-on-one meetings etc.

There should be celebration and / or acknowledgment of progress, successes, achievements and milestones. These send strong positive messages in relation to the change and reinforce its importance.

Organizations with frequent, honest and open communication policies cultivate and reinforce a culture of quality and continual improvement.

It is important to remember that accountability for the process of continual communication via various channels, in regard to a change or set of changes, lies with an individual. This does not mean that this person does all of the content creation and distribution for the change(s). Other people can have that responsibility but to ensure consistency of messaging, and avoidance of confusion, one person has to be accountable.

This is in essence a 'marketing' role associated with a change or group of changes.

Repeat

Regularly and persistently engage in the activities and behaviors deemed important to the organization to ultimately embed these in the organization's culture:

- Communicate an important change message repeatedly, frequently and widely.
- Keep communications concise, but repeat them often.
- Use multiple media formats to reach a wider audience, reinforce the message and signal its importance.
- Repeat actions and behaviors that are desirable to the organization's vision for the change.

A change in culture, and acceptance of new ways of thinking and new ways of working can take time and persistent reinforcement. Since employees learn at different rates, it makes sense to repeat a message to afford everyone time and mental space to acclimatize to fundamental changes.

Messages can be delivered in many ways including speeches from senior management, discussions at staff meetings, internal memos, newsletters and intranet systems.

Using a variety of means helps build awareness of the change in employees and also improves their understanding of the organization's plans and values.

An important aspect of repeating involves knowing when to advance to the next stage of a message or change program.

Employee surveys or other feedback tools can be used to understand how quickly a change has been adopted so that future communication and programs can be tailored appropriately.

Employees should be permitted to ask the same change questions as they learn and discover. This will allow them to fully embrace the elements of the new change.

One of the biggest mistakes many organizations make is announcing the planning of a change or the initiation of a change and then not following that up with regular and frequent updates.

This has a number of negative outcomes.

It leads to the perception that the change was just another bright idea and that nothing has happened or will happen. The next time a change is announced, people will be less receptive as they already have the perception that it is unlikely to result in anything concrete.

The other outcome is that when the change is ready for implementation, there will be increased resistance because the nature and impact of the change has not been absorbed.

The lack of regular information exchange means that employees have not been taken on the journey since the inception of the change through to its implementation.

The updates regarding change(s) should be repeated on a regular basis, across many audiences, and be clear and concise.

The more varied the media used to convey the message, the more likely you are to meet the needs of all the audiences. As mentioned in Communicate, think about the various audiences, and customize the message and the way in which it is delivered to meet the different needs of the different audiences.

This is another area to consider the use of the communication plan to help plan the message, the audience, the frequency and the medium by which it will be delivered.

It is good to try and assess how well the message regarding the change(s) is being understood or accepted. This could be done by an employee survey (and customers where appropriate) asking some key pertinent questions to help ascertain understanding and support.

Other ways in which understanding and support for the change(s) could be ascertained are through actively monitoring the questions being posed and discussions being had by employees in meetings, workshops, intranet forums, suggestion boxes and newsletters etc.

It is also beneficial to listen to watercooler and corridor conversations. What is being said in a meeting may not reflect the real sentiment of employees if there is a lack of psychological safety. See section Challenge.

Where understanding and support is not as expected, it is crucial that mitigating action is taken at the earliest opportunity to correct the situation.

See section Communicate.

Follow up

Ensure that the change tasks are completed through monitoring, reviewing and enquiring on the status of the key tasks:

- Periodically evaluate the results of the change(s).
- Obtain employee feedback to understand their level of engagement.
- Review change performance results at regular status update meetings.

As an organization evolves, it is crucial to continually assess and monitor its progress to ensure it is heading in the right direction and that employees are completing the tasks and goals assigned.

This can be achieved through feedback loops, surveys, status updates, performance dashboards and committing managers to regular communication on their change deliverables.

Regular change checkpoints should be in play so that progress, as well as employee understanding, and support can be checked. This allows timely action to be taken as soon as deviation from expected results is detected.

It is important to follow up on the progress of changes to determine whether the rate of change needs to be slowed in order to ensure tasks are completed and employees are engaged or whether it can be sped up. It is like sailing a boat. You don't just determine your current location, set a compass direction and set sail in the hope that you will reach your intended destination after a period of time.

You regularly check the compass, your current location and your progress on the journey to determine whether corrective action is needed to get the boat back on course. When there is deviation from expectation, you tack and get back on track with the intent to follow up again in a short period.

In addition to checking on progress, the goals and objectives of the change(s) should also be reviewed to ensure that they are still aligned with the overall organizational strategy. Organizations are having to evolve and change at a pace never known before so we cannot assume that organizational goals and direction have not changed as a result.

There should be a check that the goals and objectives are still relevant and have remained in line with the direction of the organization as a whole.

Where there is misalignment, corrective action should be taken to revise the goals and objectives of the change initiative(s) to bring them back in line or a decision be made to discontinue the initiative so that resources can be better allocated elsewhere.

See section Communicate.

Clarifying expectations

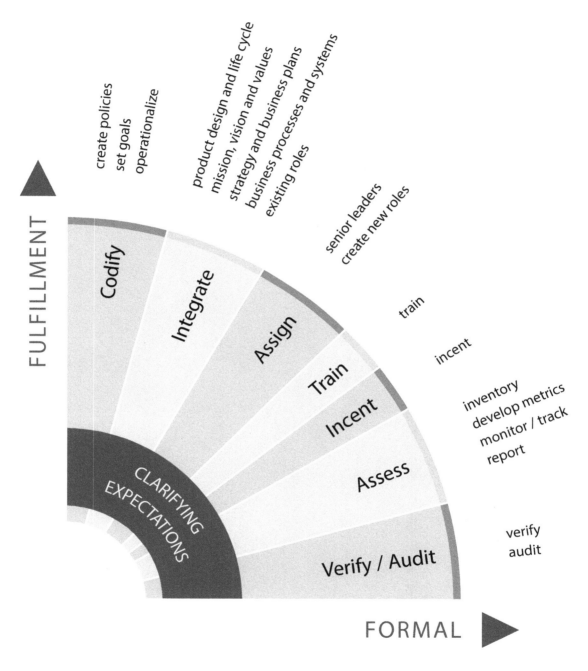

Figure 15: Clarifying expectations quadrant

While the informal practices described in the previous section will help build buy-in for the change(s), it is also important to send clear signals about how things should be done by capturing evolving behaviors and procedures in a more structured way.

The focus here is on the formal practices that support the implementation of current change initiatives.

There are seven categories of practices.

The first three categories of practice (codifying, integrating and assigning) provide the foundation for embedding the change into an organization's culture. They take the informal elements and integrate them into the core of the organization's strategies and processes.

The next set of practices (training and incentivizing) focus on formally equipping and encouraging employees via training and incentives.

The last group of practices (assessing and verifying / auditing) concentrate on determining where an organization is, measuring and tracking, and reporting on its progress as well as checking to ensure that it is on track to meet goals.

There are seven categories and eighteen practices.

QUADRANT	CATEGORY	PRACTICES
Clarifying expectations	Codify	Create policies
		Set goals
		Operationalize
	Integrate	Product, design and life cycle
		Mission, vision and values
		Strategy and business plans
		Business processes and systems
		Existing roles
	Assign	Assign responsibility to senior leadership
		Create new roles
	Train	Train
	Incent	Incent
	Assess	Inventory
		Develop metrics
		Monitor / track
		Report
	Verify / Audit	Verify
		Audit

Table 8: Clarifying expectations categories and practices

Codify

Codifying involves capturing the informal and making it explicitly formal by setting goals, creating policies, and 'operationalizing' these goals and policies in the form of practices and procedures.

The intent behind codifying is to ensure order and uniformity of purpose throughout the organization as it embarks on a cultural shift.

Codifying helps to build confidence and avoid confusion during a time of major change, by clearly spelling out the organization's position and ambitions regarding the importance of the change(s) now and in the future.

Create policies

Develop overarching organizational policies to guide behavior:

- Develop policies relating to the area of change.
- Implement codes of conduct relating to the area of the change.
- Create supplier performance policies relating to the area of the change.

Corporate policies make expected behaviors explicit and promote a set of values related to the change.

The existence of corporate policies signals the organization's commitment to the change for employees.

Establishing corporate policies, related to the area of the change, guides decision-making across the organization. Having a code of conduct related to the area of the change is a key tool for the organization to express commitment to the change. If the policies and codes of conduct are communicated effectively, it can generate a sense of managerial support of change initiatives to employees.

A policy for change(s) could include (but is not limited to) the following:

- Policy statement. A clear definition of intent and rationale e.g. the organization will use identified standards and guidelines to support the effective and efficient management of changes.
- Context. Any related policies or procedures that should be read in conjunction with this policy statement.
- Objectives. Clear objectives e.g. to adopt an industry best practice approach to change.
- Applicability. Exactly who the policy applies to and the consequences for noncompliance.
- Detailed policy statement(s). Clear concise statements that need to be complied with e.g. the organization will use the identified standards and guidelines to implement change; the organization will actively support change by the use of defined tools and resources as relevant to this policy.
- Applicable standards and guidelines. Any standards applicable to the policy and whether certification to the standard(s) is in or out of scope e.g. ISO 27001, any frameworks that are to be followed e.g. business process framework etc. and any tools to be used e.g. knowledge bases and collaboration platforms.
- Dates. Date the policy came into effect and intended duration.
- Key stakeholders. The key stakeholders associated with the policy.
- Policy authority. The highest level of management authorizing the policy e.g. CEO.
- Glossary. Definition of terms used in the policy.

Set goals

Develop organizational, departmental and individual goals and targets for the change(s):

- Set explicit organizational goals for the change.
- Set goals at the business unit and departmental levels.
- Include the area of the change in personal goal setting.
- Encourage individuals to set their own targets for the change.
- Build goals related to the change into scorecards.
- Ensure that the goals can be measured.

Goals are important and should be set at the organizational level, the level of business units and departments, and at the individual level.

Setting explicit goals and deadlines can help to coordinate activities and achieve specific targets.

All goals should be measurable. Setting ambitious targets can stimulate new ways of thinking and experimenting.

Goals should be focused and prioritized, measured via a scorecard and translated into specific actions, and teams should hold each other accountable at all times.

1. Focus

   Too many goals are just distracting and confusing. Determine which goals are the most important and critical for change success and focus on these. We need to distinguish between what is 'important' and what is 'vitally important'.

   A vitally important goal carries dire consequences if it is not achieved. Failure to achieve these goals can mean that all other achievements are rendered unimportant and of no value.

2. Scorecard

   When you are keeping score, you have people's attention. If employees cannot see how success is being measured, the goals will be unclear. Measures also mean that everyone is on the same page. Without supporting measures, a goal could be interpreted differently by every employee. Scorecards are compelling, visible and accessible and critical to change success.

3. Be specific

   Goals have to be turned into specific actions otherwise they remain lofty aspirations. Achieving new goals means doing thing differently. Everyone needs to understand the actions they need to take to achieve the goal.

4. Accountability

   Everyone on a team needs to hold each other accountable. Teams that achieve success are the ones that meet on a regular basis, examine the scorecard, discuss issues and agree how they are going to be resolved, and provide ongoing support for each other. If there is no accountability, there will be no progress.

Scorecards

Scorecards could include a balanced scorecard as developed by Dr. Robert Kaplan and Dr. David Norton in the early 1990s.

Essentially, the balanced scorecard (BSC) specifies that we should view the organization from four different perspectives (or quadrants): learning and growth, internal business process, customer and financial.

Metrics are then produced, and data / information collected and analyzed in respect to each quadrant.

The first step is to ensure there is an understanding of the business goals and objectives and that the goals and objectives of the change(s) are aligned before populating the BSC.

A series of questions can help determine what should be measured and managed using the BSC. Those questions are:

Financial:	To succeed financially, how should we appear to our stakeholders?
Customer:	To achieve our vision, how should we appear to our customers?
Learning and growth:	To achieve our vision, how will we sustain our ability to innovate, improve and grow?
Business processes:	To meet the needs of our stakeholders and customers, what processes must we excel at?

Answering these questions can then help determine what should be measured using the BSC. Every scorecard will be unique depending on the organizational goals and objectives.

Therefore, the following table is an example change scorecard providing some hypothetical answers to the questions. Each of these answers then becomes an element that can be assessed, measured and managed.

FINANCIAL	CUSTOMER
To succeed financially, how should we appear to our stakeholders?	*To achieve our vision, how should we appear to our customers?*
• Economic service provision.	• Increased customer satisfaction.
• Effective supplier management.	• Improved availability of services.
• Understanding our costs to the rest of business.	• Increased reliability of services.
	• Provision of self-help and empowerment for customers.
LEARNING AND GROWTH	**BUSINESS PROCESSES**
To achieve our vision, how will we sustain our ability to innovate, improve and grow?	*To meet the needs of our stakeholders and customers, what processes must we excel at?*
• Manage service and product innovation.	• Lower process costs.
• Attract, acquire and retain skilled and motivated employees.	• Compliance with industry standards, regulations and legislation.
	• Accountability for service provision.

Table 9: Example balanced scorecard

The overall scorecard for changes(s) can then be cascaded through the organization.

Individual areas can define additional measures and targets that support the overall goals and targets of changes(s).

The following table is an example of a contact center scorecard that supports the overall change improvement BSC.

This BSC contains the goal related to the change improvement BSC quadrants as well as associated key performance indicators (KPIs), metrics and initiatives to be put in place to achieve those goals.

	GOAL	KPI	METRIC	INITIATIVE
FINANCIAL	Decrease contact center costs.	Decrease cost of onboarding agents.	Decrease completion of onboarding by 10% over 12-month period.	Use AI to monitor platform usage and educate real time.
CUSTOMER	Customer satisfaction.	Increase customer satisfaction with the contact center.	Increase customer satisfaction rating in surveys to 7.5.	Increased training. Increased self-help. Leverage technology.
LEARNING AND GROWTH	Business and productivity.	Introduce new ways for customers to access the contact center.	Introduce two new methods for interaction in 12-month period.	Use of chatbots, self-help, AI and increased monitoring of social media channels.
BUSINESS PROCESSES	Decreased time to resolve customer issues.	Minimize mean time to resolution.	Decrease time to resolve customer issues by 15% over 12-month period.	Increased knowledge articles and use of technology.

Table 10: Example contact center balanced scorecard

A key thing to remember is that if you can't measure something, then you can't manage it. For example, if you don't know the cost of onboarding a contact center agent today, you can't determine whether you have reduced that by 10% in 12 months as per the metric in the BSC.

A baseline must be established that can be continually monitored and measured so that (a) achievable targets can be set (b) progress against those targets can be measured and (c) achievement of targets can be demonstrated.

Operationalize

Develop the standards, procedure and practices that enact corporate policies, and translate goals and policies into work practices:

- Translate abstract objectives into everyday work practices.
- Develop procedures and standards related to the change.

Employees can deliver on change objectives more easily if they are built into daily operations and practices. The development of detailed standards and procedures clarifies and reinforces expected behaviors. In short, this practice is about translating ideas into desired actions.

The lack of effort to link change initiatives to daily operations is one of the main causes of inaction and a key hindrance in implementing change.

Enacted formalized policies embed the change into the organizational culture.

However, that culture is weakened when policies are undermined by a lack of supporting management practices and when punishment, rather than reward, is used.

Moving from policies and goals to execution and delivery on desired outcomes requires alignment, commitment and cohesion across the entire organization.

When we talk about operationalization of polices and goals, we are referring to the establishment of objectives, allocation of resources, and development of functional targets and delivery.

Achievement of goals requires planning and allocation of tasks. Leadership teams schedule the work needed to complete the tasks on the plan. They actively track the metrics that show the value being delivered by the plan and assuring that movement toward achievement of the goals is being made. If desired progress is not being made, adjustments are made accordingly.

The objectives for the tasks should be SMART objectives. See section Develop metrics.

The operationalized plan has to engage everyone in the organization, not just the executive leadership. As leaders roll out the plan, they link the tasks back to the achievement of organizational goals.

Resource allocation allows for a plan to be executed and it is usually an executive team that decides which organizational units (e.g. divisions, departments, business units or teams) will receive finances, facilities and executive support.

Regular measurement and monitoring are fundamental to success.

The operationalized plan becomes a lens for the organization to view new opportunities, risks and decisions. As opportunities present themselves, questions can be asked to determine alignment with the current plan:

- Does this opportunity fit with the context of our current goals and plan?
- Does this opportunity support achievement of our goals?
- Are we still aligned with the achievement of our goals?

An operationalized plan allows leadership teams to make informed decisions. The plan sets the direction and everything else should be measured against, aligned with, or driven by the plan.

The plan has to be flexible, and easily changed and adjusted as needed. Changes in the external and internal environment will happen and the plan may need to be adapted accordingly.

Integrate

Integrate is the formal integration of the change into the way the organization currently operates. This includes incorporating the change into the organization's mission, vision and values, strategy, business plans, business processes, roles, management systems, product design and life cycle.

Through this integration, an organization truly commits to transformation by incorporating change(s) into its core.

Product design and life cycle

Integrate the change into the life cycle of all products and services delivered by the organization:

- Assess the impact of the change on the life cycle of products and services.
- Embed the change into the life cycle of products and services.

An organization's products and services are the core artefacts of its existence.

Employees and other stakeholders often see the organization and its products / services as inseparable.

Addressing product / service design is an important signal to employees that the organization can successfully deliver on its vision.

Organizational change initiatives will have an impact on the entire life cycle and supply chain for products and services. These need to be embedded at every stage of the life cycle from product / service initiation, design and development, build and test, and operation / provision through to retirement.

Let's look at an organizational change initiative to increase environmental sustainability and how that impacts product design. An organization wishes to weave sustainable design into an existing process to ensure that it becomes embedded within the organization.

This means that consideration has to be given to:

1. Raw material extraction
2. Manufacturing and processing
3. Transportation
4. Usage and retail
5. Waste disposal.

Product design consideration will vary between design approaches but there are common principles that include the following:

- Change the use of traditional materials to ones that have a lower environmental impact such as non-toxic, sustainably produced or recycled materials.
- Use manufacturing processes that are more energy efficient.
- Create products that are more energy efficient.
- Create products that are longer lasting and have components that have to be replaced less frequently.
- Design products for reuse and recycling wherein the component parts can be disassembled and reused to make other products.
- Consult design and environmental standards and guides e.g. ISO/IEC Guide 41:2018 Packaging – Recommendations for addressing consumer needs.
- Use life cycle analysis (LCA) tools to help design more sustainable products.
- Shift the consumption mode from personal ownership of products to provision of services that provide similar functions. Some examples of companies that have made this change are Xerox (copier leasing rather than purchase), and GoGet (car sharing).
- Materials should come from nearby, sustainably managed, renewable sources that can be composted when their usefulness is exhausted.

All of these principles would have to be embedded into the product design life cycle to integrate the change regarding increased environmental sustainability.

Mission, vision and values

Incorporate values related to the change into the organization's mission, vision and values.

- Establish a new mission if one does not already exist or if it does not explicitly address the area of change.
- Update the organizational vision to reflect what it would be like if the change was fully implemented and upheld.
- Incorporate the area of the change into the organization's values.
- Increase the level of the areas of the change among the organization's values if appropriate.

An organization's mission, vision and values are formal, overarching statements of commitment that send a clear message to its employees and other stakeholders about its position in relation to the change.

Integration of the change into these areas holds everyone from board members to employees accountable for their actions and encourages employees to take the change area into account when making decisions.

Clear articulation within the mission, vision and values may also foster an alignment within the organization. By integrating the area of change into the mission, vision and values, an organization can inspire and motivate employees to take obligations to the next level and enables leadership to challenge their people to do something great.

Encourage teams to develop their own mission statement in relation to the change to build a sense of collective ownership, commitment and focus.

Guidance on the creation of mission statements includes:

Keep them simple. Use common language. Be authentic.

Make them compelling. Present a common purpose. Inspire. Ensure employees can relate to it.

Make them measurable. This can be a tough one but a statement like 'Customers can find and discover anything they might want to buy online' can be measured.

Enduring. You do not want to be rewriting your mission statement on a regular basis so make sure it is enduring and can remain relevant.

Here are some mission statements that contain values related to a change around sustainability.

"Our company's foundation is built on our values, which distinguish us and guide our actions. We conduct our business in a socially responsible and ethical manner. We respect the law, support universal human rights, protect the environment and benefit the communities where we work."—Chevron[5]

"We will continue to drive initiatives that promote equality, inclusion and opportunities for our partners. We will continue to support bringing people together in service and working to address complex problems in our communities. And we will continue to make sustainability a priority as we have for more than 30 years, from ethically and sustainably sourcing coffee to building greener stores."—Starbucks[6]

"We will integrate environmental and social principles in our businesses, ensuring that what comes from the people goes back to the people many times over."—TATA Group[7]

Strategy and business plans

Incorporate the change into the organization's strategic planning process:

- Prioritize the area of change in the strategic planning process.
- Incorporate the area of change into strategy.
- Involve those responsible for implementing the change in the formulation of a new strategy.
- Emphasize the change area as a strategic priority.
- Directly integrate change goals and deadlines into individual business unit's business plans.
- Require that business units address the change in their business plans.

Organizations should integrate the change across all-functions as appropriate.

They should explicitly consider the change area when reconfiguring their strategic planning process and include the individuals responsible for implementing the change in corporate strategic planning.

Once the strategic goals have been set, the next step is to incorporate the change into the organization's various business plans. This will bring these goals down to the next level of business units or of particular products or services (depending on how the organization structures its business planning). This can take the form of requiring business units to identify how they will contribute to the organization's overall goals (relating to the change) or asking them to set unit-level targets (relating to the change).

Here is a simple approach to cascading a strategic plan:

1. Create a strategic plan incorporating values related to the change.
2. Cascade to different units: divisions, departments and teams.
3. Units create their own strategic plan to align with the larger strategic plan.
4. Units plan how they will move their goals and priorities forward to fulfill the plan.

Business processes and systems

Incorporate the change into existing business tools and processes:

*   Fully integrate the change throughout existing business tools and processes.
*   Build metrics related to the change into day-to-day business processes.
*   Adapt management systems to identify and manage issues related to the area of change.
*   Enhance decision support systems based on factors relating to the area of change.

Moving from strategy to planning takes us into the realm of business processes and tools. Organizations are increasingly turning to various types of management systems to manage complex business processes or to track and analyze data.

Given that business processes and systems drive day-to-day operations and decision- making, organizations should embed the change within these areas in order to drive and support the change. This could include existing processes such as health and safety systems, systems management systems, service management systems, environmental management systems and total quality management systems etc.

Incorporating the change goals and metrics into business processes and systems can help support systemic improvements.

The integration of changes into business processes and systems ensures that change becomes business as usual. The change becomes integral to the way the organization operates.

Changes have to be integrated into processes and systems so that the changes become fundamental to how employees work. The degree of integration will depend on the nature of the change. For example, let's consider a change that involves moving from a workplace full of like-minded individuals to one comprised of diversity—a workplace of diverse knowledge, opinions and experience. This is an organization where diversity and inclusivity are desired.

This change will need to address a number of processes and systems that may include:

*   Recruitment
*   Hiring
*   Onboarding and initiation
*   Employee assistance program
*   Reward and recognition
*   Performance management
*   Training
*   Communication
*   Organizational structure.

Existing roles

Add responsibilities and expectations related to the area of change to the description of every role in the organization:

- Change staff job descriptions to incorporate the change.
- Assign tasks to roles, not people.

This practice focuses on the integration of the change at an individual level. Once the organization has defined and integrated the change into its mission, vision and values, it can translate this vision into individual roles at all levels of the organization, from CEO down.

Making the change part of the role description for every function in the organization ensures that it becomes part of everyone's day-to-day work.

Coupled with role descriptions, organizations need to ensure that employees know how their performance will be measured. Accountability mechanisms need to be fair and effective to maintain ongoing improvement.

Changes to job descriptions, as a result of a change initiative, can serve to raise awareness of the area of change and increase employee engagement with the change as it now relates directly to their job.

A good place to start with roles is the creation of a RACI matrix.

RACI stands for responsible, accountable, consulted and informed. A RACI matrix allows for the identification of the activities within a process and the roles and responsibilities associated with each of these activities.

Once the roles and responsibilities have been identified, they can then be incorporated into associated job descriptions and the metrics by which the effective performance of those activities will be measured will be determined so that they can be included in performance scorecards etc.

The RACI matrix is also known as the responsibility assignment matrix (RAM) or linear responsibility chart (LRC). It describes the level of participation of a given role in a process.

The definitions are as follows:

Responsible: This applies to those who do the work to achieve the activity.

Accountable: This is applied to the ONE role that is ultimately accountable for the achievement of the activity. This is often referred to as 'the buck stops here'. For each activity, there can only be one accountable entry is the matrix.

Consulted: This applies to those whose opinions and input are sought and where there is two-way communication.

Informed: This applies to those who are kept up to date on progress and it is just a one-way communication.

A role may be both accountable and responsible for a particular activity.

The following is an example of an RACI matrix that may be created to determine the roles and activities to hold an organizational event to launch a change.

	Project sponsor	Project manager	Facilities	Guest team	Venue owner	Catering	Media
Request	A/R	C					
Ideas	C	A/R	C	C			
Develop	C	A/R	C	C	C	C	
Plan	C	A/R	C	C	C		
Venue	I	A	R		C		
Catering		A	R	C	C	C	
Guests	A	A	C	R			
Program	I	A/R	C	C	I	I	C
Monitor	C/I	A/R	C	C	C	C	C
Event	I	A/R	C	C	C	C	C
Review	C	A/R	C	C			

Table 11: Example RACI matrix

Assign

Practices in this category involve allocating responsibility for the change to new or existing roles within the organization including roles at the most senior levels.

This may include the creation of new roles within organizations to address new responsibilities, including managing compliance to the change, dealing with stakeholders (including employees), tracking and reporting on progress, and leading change innovation.

Organizations can create new roles, and hold senior leaders and board members accountable for change deliverables. By assigning responsibility for the change to specific roles at senior levels, the organization signals that the change is a priority.

Assign responsibility to senior leadership

Allocate the responsibility of delivering on the change agenda to senior leadership roles within the organization:

- Assign responsibility for the change to board members and / or a board subcommittee.
- Assign responsibility for the change to the CxO.
- Assign responsibility for the change to roles within the senior leadership (e.g. create a VP for service management or a VP for sustainability).

Actions taken by senior leadership send very strong signals to the rest of the organization. When senior leadership takes direct responsibility for a change, the commitment to the change is transferred down through the organization.

We often hear reference to Professor John P. Kotter's 'guiding coalition', which first appeared in his book *Leading Change. The guiding coalition was a group assembled with enough power to lead a change, guide it, coordinate it and communicate its activities.*

This was often comprised of senior leadership and focused on one change. Change is now constant in organizations and increasing in speed and agility. A guiding coalition for every change is no longer feasible.

While I agree that a dedicated guiding coalition is still required for major and transformational change within an organization, I believe there is also a guiding coalition needed to oversee all changes. This guiding coalition is a group of enthusiastic volunteers, including leaders, who are advocates for constant change across the entire organization.

Their role includes increasing awareness and understanding that constant change is the norm for the organization if it is to remain relevant. They are change champions and come from all parts of the organization. They are diverse with unique skills, perspectives and networks. This composition allows them to see all sides of an opportunity or issue and enable innovative ideas to emerge. Their varied roles and titles give them the needed credibility to champion change efforts at all levels of the organization and their passion maintains momentum and capacity for change.

Create new roles

Expand existing roles or develop new roles within the organization to capture essential responsibilities relating to the change:

- Assign full-time personnel to lead the change program(s).
- Create new roles to deliver on the change agenda.
- Create a department with prime responsibility for the change (e.g. sustainability office, change management office, health and safety office, continual improvement office).
- Expand or upgrade existing roles to incorporate the change.
- Give these roles direct exposure to senior leadership.
- Ensure these roles do not operate in isolation but collaborate and integrate with the rest of the organization (e.g. through cross-functional teams).

The creation of specific roles in relation to the area of change has a legitimizing effect within the organization. Failure to create roles and assign responsibility will stand in the way of effective implementation of change programs. Assigning responsibility for the area of the change to roles within the organization, and prioritizing the importance of those roles, demonstrates management commitment to the change to employees and other stakeholders.

Train

Training provides employees with the additional skills and knowledge to help them accomplish tasks, work with systems, or carry out procedures related to or involving the change.

Training clarifies expectations and creates consistency in behaviors.

Train

Train employees in systems or procedures related to the change:

- Include training related to the change in employee induction programs.
- Provide ongoing training / refresh programs in relation to the change.
- Maintain training programs in line with new change initiatives.

Training can be effective in embedding a change within the organization. Training should be repeated on a regular basis and an assessment of the effectiveness of the training carried out immediately following the training and after a period of elapsed time. Improvement to training programs can then be identified and implemented.

Training is not only integral to gaining new skills but also:

- For bringing employees together around a central focus in order to build cohesion and commitment.
- For developing employees' skills in human interaction.
- For showing management commitment to innovation through the organization's investment in time and resources for the purpose of acquiring new skills and ideas that support teamwork.

Training needs analysis

Determining training needs is undertaken using a training needs analysis (TNA).

A TNA reviews learning and development needs across the organization. It will consider knowledge, skills and behaviors that employees need and how to develop them effectively. A TNA will not only do this for training in regard to the change(s) in play but also to determine how to bridge the gap between the skills the organization has today and those it has determined it will need in the future.

A TNA means that appropriate, efficient and cost-effective training is delivered to meet the needs of the employee and the organization.

There are many software systems that will undertake a TNA for you, saving time and often money.

The underlying steps, however, remain the same.

1. Understand the learning objectives desired outcomes

   Define the outcomes you want to see. Determine how you will measure achievement of those outcomes. The goal of the training should relate to business objectives e.g. the adoption of a change or developing skills for the future.

2. Identify the required skills and knowledge

    Identify the skills and knowledge that employees will require to achieve the defined goal and outcomes. These should be the critical competencies including behaviors, knowledge, skills and personal traits that are linked to the goals and outcomes.

    This is a good time to involve employees and ask them what they think they need. This engages them in the process and understanding of the objectives.

3. Assessment and gap analysis

    An assessment of current abilities in relation to the required skills needs to take place. There are many ways to conduct the assessment including (but not limited to):

    »   Direct observation
    »   Questionnaires
    »   Consultation key personnel
    »   Review of relevant literature
    »   Interviews
    »   Focus groups
    »   Assessments / surveys
    »   Records and report studies
    »   Work samples.

    Determine the gap between the current abilities and the desired abilities. The data collected should show where the gaps exist. Create a list of gaps and prioritize them in order of importance.

4. Evaluate current offerings

    Evaluate the training offerings that are currently available within the organization and whether they will be sufficient to address the gaps. The evaluation may reveal areas where existing training will address the gaps if improved or revised. It may be discovered that there are training materials available but the way in which they are deployed needs to be addressed. For example, online training courses are available, but they cannot currently be accessed via mobile devices.

5. Training plan

    Develop a training plan that may include the following:

    »   Define the learning outcomes
    »   Training structure
    »   Develop the content (if training is to be provided internally)
    »   Identify training providers (if training is to be sourced externally)
    »   Training recipients
    »   Time frames
    »   Delivery method(s)
    »   Training duration
    »   Training evaluation methods and measurement.

6. Implement

    Implement the plan and incorporate regular feedback loops (from students, trainers, managers, etc.) to continually assess the effectiveness of the training.

Training methods

The type of training you choose will be based on many considerations including budget and time constraints. What needs to be given careful consideration is the preferred learning style(s) of the employees so that the method chosen delivers the best return on investment.

Training methods may include:

- Lecture or presentation
- Workshop or discussion
- Computer based training (CBT)
- Web based training (WBT)
- Simulations or experiential learning
- On-the-job training
- Virtually delivered training
- Books
- Conferences
- Mentoring and coaching.

When selecting the most appropriate training method(s), remember that when employees perform a task as part of a training program, they retain an average of 75% of information compared to just 5% when learning in a passive environment such as a lecture.

Incent

Incentives encourage employee commitment and involvement with change initiatives.

It should be noted that this category is referring to the formal practice of providing financial incentives as opposed to the informal practice of providing recognition discussed in section Fostering commitment.

Incent

Link compensation to the achievement of set objectives related to the change:

- Include metrics related to the change in employees' performance appraisal and assessment.
- Link compensation to performance related to the change.
- Redesign promotion, salary increases and benefits to reward good performance.
- Be clear how people will be measured and ensure that achievement of the targets is within that person's control.

When something is built into the pay / bonus structure of the organization, it gets incorporated into everyday business more quickly. Targets that were previously described as unattainable are suddenly reached in the presence of financial incentives.

Financially rewarding employees for their personal contribution toward change initiatives encourages them to participate in activities and recognizes those who participate over those who do not.

The key is to be open and transparent about the data being used to assess bonuses; making assessments cumulative (based on performance trends over time); and in cases of missed targets, making a distinction between system failures and individual failures.

Research has shown that performance-related pay is positively associated with job satisfaction, organizational commitment and trust in management.[8] Profit-related pay did not have the same effect.

Other considerations, in regard to incentives to adopt change supported by research, are:

99% of employees have unique reward preferences, which make incentives a good alternative to a traditional reward system.[9]

78% of employees are willing to remain with their current employer due to the competitive perks and incentives it offers.[10]

90% of the highest performing companies use incentives and rewards to retain and encourage employees.[11]

According to FutureFuel.io, the best 23 ranked (2020) employee incentive programs are[12]:

1. Customized paid vacation
2. Green transport
3. On-site entertainment
4. Unlimited sick leave
5. Free online skill development courses
6. Free e-learning programs
7. One-on-one mentorship
8. Fast food catering on specific weekdays
9. Free healthy snacks
10. Stationery and equipment personalization
11. Health programs
12. Club and society membership
13. Rest and relaxation rooms
14. Streaming subscriptions
15. Department / team activities
16. Gamification of tasks
17. Profit sharing among employees
18. Working remotely, whenever
19. Elimination of degree requirements
20. Unlimited medical insurance coverage
21. Vehicle financing assistance
22. Consumer goods financing assistance
23. Student loan debt assistance.

Employee incentives to adopt change can help overcome inertia and reluctance to change as long as the required change in behavior is clear. It should also be absolutely clear what behaviors are being incentivized and the incent should be given in a timely manner in regard to the change taking place.

Assess

The practices in this category relate to understanding where the organization is, where it wants to go and whether it is on track to get there. The practices also deal with developing an awareness of an organization's capability for change and an understanding of how much change is required.

Assessment practices also involve measuring and tracking performance and documenting progress.

The practices (taking inventory, developing metrics, monitoring / tracking and reporting) attempt to address these issues.

Inventory

Develop an understanding of where an organization is, where it may lead and where it may lag. Conduct base-line assessments:

- Survey employees to understand their attitudes.
- Critically assess the organization's strengths and weaknesses.
- Critically assess the organization's readiness for change.
- Critically assess the maturity of processes and process areas.

It is important to develop a baseline before charging ahead with change initiatives. Activities can include an annual survey of employees to see whether they are engaged in the change initiatives; assessing employee and organizational readiness for change; assessing the current maturity of specific processes or process areas and performing a gap analysis; assessing the organization against certifiable standards such as ISO/IEC 20000, ISO 14001 etc.

Baseline assessments should be repeated on a regular basis so that progress against defined targets can be measured and new baselines established.

Attitudes

Employee attitude surveys are useful tools in providing information in regard to how employees view the organization and organizational change.

Note that employee attitudes toward change are positively related to employee readiness for change.

The following is an example of survey questions that could be used to assess attitudes to change.

Survey recipients are asked to score either a 1, 2 or 3 and to choose the answer they believe is MOST reflective of the organization.

Question	Answers			Score
How change resistant is the organization?	**1** Open to change	**2** Partially	**3** Highly resistant to change	
How much change is currently taking place?	**1** No change	**2** Medium amount of change	**3** Large amount of change	
Were past changes seen as positive or negative experiences?	**1** Positive	**2** Partially	**2** Negative	
How does management reward people?	**1** For embracing change and risk taking	**2** Somewhere in between	**3** For consistency and maintaining the status quo	
Are adequate resources available for change initiatives?	**1** Yes	**2** Sometimes	**3** No	
Is there a clear vision for the organization?	**1** Yes	**2** Partially	**3** No	
Do we effectively communicate the reason for change throughout the change life cycle (i.e. from conception through to post-implementation)?	**1** Yes	**2** Partially	**3** No	
Are those responsible for the implementation of the change highly respected with a successful track record?	**1** Yes	**2** Partially	**3** No	
Are sponsors (those managers needed to be advocates for the change and to authorize it) highly respected with a successful track record?	**1** Yes	**2** Partially	**3** No	
TOTAL SCORE				

Once completed, the scores from each survey should be collated and an average determined based on the number of surveys returned.

The following score ranges will inform you of employees' attitude to change and whether they are open to change or resistance to change.

LOW 1–10: This indicates an organization that is open to change and embracing improvements. There is an environment and capability to support a successful improvement initiative. The initiative is low in risk from an organizational change management perspective. There will be less of a need for organizational change management resources and effort than for an improvement initiative scoring in the following two categories.

In regard to the Balanced Diversity framework, fewer practices may be chosen from the framework, as there is a higher likelihood that the organization will embrace the change. For example, it may not be necessary to use practices from the 'reenvision' category as there is a shared vision and goals in place for the organization that are understood.

MEDIUM 11–20: This indicates an organization that is midway between one that is highly resistant to improvement and change and one that is open to change. There is a mixture of capability and perception of past improvement initiatives. Work will need to take place to determine where the pockets of resistance exist, and organizational change management plans will need to address those pockets of resistance. Identifying the pockets of resistance and the causes of that resistance will help in the selection of practices. For example, in regard to the Balanced Diversity framework, if the pockets of resistance are coming from a team that does not feel it has been adequately involved or consulted in previous improvement initiatives, then you may choose practices from the 'communicate' and 'invite' categories to make sure those issues are addressed.

HIGH 20–30: This indicates a highly change resistant organization with a poor history of improvement initiatives and a low organizational change management competency. The organizational change management plans will need to address resistance to change and more effort and resources will be required from an organizational change management perspective. This may drive the choice of more practices from the framework than an improvement initiative scoring in the prior two categories. In regard to the Balanced Diversity framework, to overcome resistance, practices from 'raise awareness', 'communicate', 'integrate' and 'learn' may be chosen. For example, if resistance is due to past improvement initiatives being seen as negative, the 'learn from failure' practice in the 'learn' category is likely to be selected.

Strengths and weaknesses

Organizational strengths and weakness can be assessed using a SWOT analysis (strengths, weaknesses, opportunities and threats).

When you know the strengths, weaknesses, opportunities and threats of the organization, you can plan and act more effectively for change.

SWOT analysis explores both internal and external factors that might influence change success.

The following is an example template for conducting the SWOT analysis.

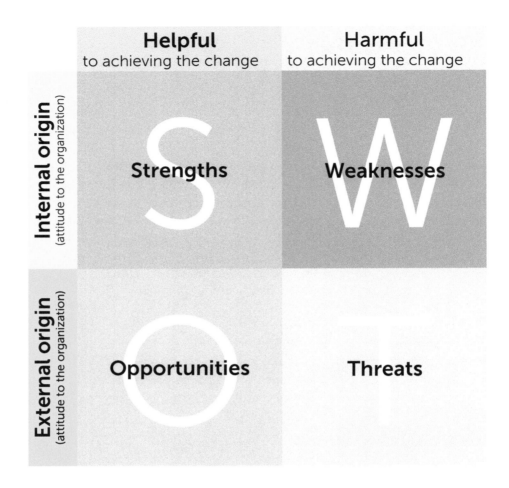

Figure 16: SWOT analysis template example

Ask those participating in the analysis to answer these questions: What are the strengths and weaknesses of the organization? What are the opportunities and threats facing it?

Internal factors: strengths and weaknesses

These could include (but are not limited to):

- Employees: executive, management, staff
- Infrastructure: location, buildings, equipment, technology
- Finance: grants, funds, sources of income
- Products and services
- Past experiences of change.

External factors: opportunities and threats

These could include (but are not limited to):

- Future trends in the industry
- Economy: local, national and international
- Funding sources
- Demographics: changes in age, race and gender within the organization

- Physical environment / location
- Legislation and regulation
- Local, national and international events
- Competition.

Readiness for change

Data collection to determine readiness for change should use both qualitative and quantitative methods.

Qualitative data is collected via interview with those people most directly connected or impacted by the change.

Quantitative data is collected via a change readiness survey. This will go to a much larger group than that covered by interview.

The following interview and survey questions are reproduced with permission of **Dashe and Thomson.**[13]

Interview questions are conducted at the leadership level.

Interview

1. Can you explain how this (change initiative) fits with the strategic goals of your organization?
2. How well do you feel the rationale for the change has been communicated to the organization?
3. Can you explain what you are hearing from key stakeholders (users, clients, customers—internal or external, or regulatory agencies) about the need for this change?
4. What are you hearing from your users about change progress to date?
5. What are you hearing from your peers about this change e.g. other company leadership or steering committee members?
6. How will you measure success for this change?
7. We often talk about the triple constraint: Time, Cost and Quality. Some people say, "you can have two, but not three." So far, how would you rank the order of importance the organization has placed on each of these three constraints? For example: "The organization has cut the project budget, but kept scope the same, so the priorities would appear to be 1) cost 2) quality and 3) time."
8. What has the organization's past experience been with change?
9. What do you see as the major risks for the project?
10. How do you normally communicate with employees in your organization?
11. What messages have you put out, to date, about this change?
12. What other issues should I know about that we have not discussed?

The information learned during these interviews is vital. Some examples of outcomes that can be revealed include:

- A level of understanding of the change rationale.
- A level of understanding of the benefits and barriers that the change will present.
- Whether the change vision has been appropriately disseminated to stakeholders.
- A baseline understanding of the company's appetite for change.

Survey

As the survey goes to a larger audience (leadership, project team, change team and end users), it can reveal areas that need specific focus and any level of misalignment between leadership and end users.

The survey uses a mix of questions, asking the stakeholder to rate how much they agree with the statement on a scale of 1 to 5 (with 5 being strongly agree and 1 being don't agree at all).

1. The change sponsor has a clear vision of where we are going with this change.
2. The change sponsor has shown a clear commitment to making the change happen.
3. Key executives clearly support the change.
4. Project leaders and executives have made it clear that the change is aligned with the company's strategic goals.
5. It is clear what my department has to do to make the change succeed.
6. My department has sufficient resources (people, training, support) to help the change succeed.
7. My department has a plan to get ready for the changes.
8. The change stays on track, despite other corporate / organizational priorities that may come up.
9. My management is committed to making the change a success.
10. The change is receiving priority in my department.
11. I understand how my role will be affected by the change.
12. We get regular change updates that indicate what progress we are making toward our goals.
13. The reason for change has been explained to my department.
14. We are following a detailed plan.
15. Changes to business processes have been explained to my department.
16. People who embrace change and innovation are rewarded for their efforts.
17. People share problems and concerns with leadership rather than keeping them quiet or hiding them.
18. Key technology partners are delivering on what they promised.
19. Our present organizational culture can support the way we will do things in the future.
20. I believe I will be ready for this change.

The combination of the results from both the interviews and survey provides data that informs the overall change readiness assessment report. Analysis of the data provides a road map for change and communication tactics to best serve the needs of the business.

Analyzing data across business units allows tailoring of communication to those units.

Heat maps can be created to highlight the areas / departments that need more focus or support.

Question	People and Culture	Legal	Marketing	Operations
1. The change sponsor has a clear vision of where we are going with this change.	4.31	4.00	3.83	4.00
2. The change sponsor has shown a clear commitment to making the change happen.	4.48	4.25	3.93	5.00
3. Key executives clearly support the change.	4.26	4.15	4.09	3.00
4. Change leaders and executives have made it clear that the change is aligned with the company's strategic goals.	4.35	4.10	4.06	4.00
5. It is clear what my department has to do to make the change succeed.	4.08	3.33	3.16	2.00

Figure 17: Example heat map

Analysis of all the data collected will provide a road map for change and communication tactics to best serve the needs of the organization.

Process maturity

Undertaking a measurement of process maturity indicates the organization's commitment to improvement.

Maturity assessments provide a baseline from which improvement can be measured. They help identify the areas to which improvement activities should be focused. Rather than a scattergun approach to process improvement, maturity assessments inform a targeted approach ensuring resources are allocated where they are best needed.

Assessments can be conducted internally by employees within the organization or by an external party. There are clearly pros and cons to each. Internal assessments often cost less to conduct but there can be a lack of objectivity and impartiality. External assessments, while more expensive, can remove the subjectivity and are undertaken by subject matter experts who can provide an accurate maturity rating based on their in-depth knowledge of the processes in scope and the maturity framework being used for assessment.

One of the most commonly used approaches to process maturity assessment is the Capability Maturity Model Integration (CMMI), which is administered by the CMMI Institute and was developed at Carnegie Mellon University (CMU).

CMMI defines five maturity levels as show in this table.

Score	Name	Description
1	Initial	Processes at this level are (typically) undocumented and are in a state of dynamic change, tending to be driven in an ad hoc, uncontrolled and reactive manner by users or events. This provides a chaotic or unstable environment for the processes.
2	Repeatable	At this level, some processes are repeatable, possibly with consistent results. Process discipline is unlikely to be rigorous, but where it exists it may help to ensure that existing processes are maintained during times of stress.
3	Defined	At this level, there are sets of defined and documented standard processes established and subject to some degree of improvement over time. These standard processes are in place (i.e. the AS-IS processes) and used to establish consistency of process performance across the organization.
4	Managed	It is characteristic of processes at this level that using process metrics, management can effectively control the AS-IS process (e.g. for software development). In particular, management can identify ways to adjust and adapt the process to particular projects without measurable losses of quality or deviations from specifications. Process capability is established from this level.
5	Optimized	At this level, the focus is on continually improving process performance through incremental and innovative technological changes / improvements.

Table 12: CMMI maturity levels

Organizations cannot be certified in CMMI. Instead, they are *appraised* and awarded a maturity level rating (1–5) or a capability level achievement profile which is a list of processes and their corresponding capability level.

The outputs from an assessment may include the production of spider diagrams that indicate the process maturity against various elements (e.g. people, technology, culture etc.)

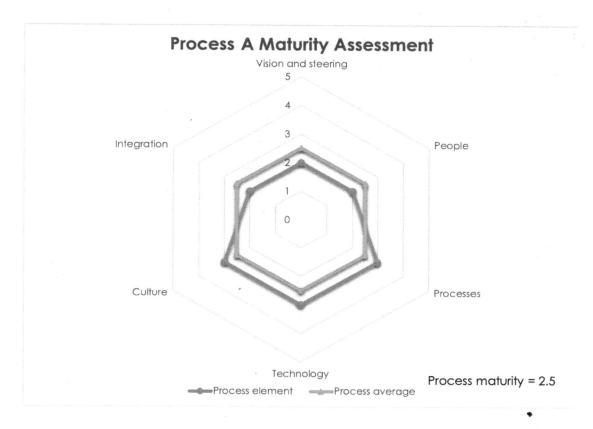

Figure 18: Example maturity assessment spider diagram

Develop metrics

Develop ways to measure progress toward the change goal. This is the process of deciding what to track in order to monitor progress:

- Translate ambiguous and poorly defined concepts into tangible objectives and metrics appropriate for the organization's products and services.
- Identify all forms of relevant change data to be monitored and collected.
- Use discussions and negotiations over metrics as a way to refine collective understandings, goals and priorities.

Developing metrics can be seen as one way of operationalizing the change.

Organizations can use discussions and negotiations over metrics as a way to refine collective understandings, to set goals and to define priorities. Organizations should define consistent metrics that are tailored and relevant to them. Performance metrics should be reliable and meaningful. Development of relevant metrics is needed for an organization to track its achievements.

Metrics should be SMART (specific, measurable, achievable, realistic and timely). Ask the following questions of each of the metrics you propose to measure change progress / performance.

Is the metric **specific**? Does it measure a specific process or part of a process?

Is the metric **measurable**? Do you have the capability to measure? Do you have the resources—people, tools, technology etc.?

Is the metric **achievable**? Do not set a target that is completely unachievable. Stretch targets are good but they should still be achievable.

Is the metric **realistic**? Does the metric make sense in the 'real-world'?

Is the metric **timely**? Is the measurement of the right frequency and regularity to support effective decision-making? A measure that is not taken regularly enough could mean that deviations from expected progress toward a goal is not detected early enough for corrective action to be taken. A measurement that is taken too often could give the perception that no or little progress is being made and this can have a detrimental impact on morale.

Organizational change management is ultimately considered with people, their emotions and behaviors. As a result, these are often hard complex issues and hard to measure accurately.

Regardless of the difficulty, measuring the effectiveness of change efforts, both quantitatively and qualitatively, is fundamental to success.

You cannot manage what you cannot measure.

One tool that can be used to measure change progress is the ADKAR® model from Prosci®.

ADKAR® is a framework used to understand change at the individual level and how organizations can increase the likelihood that change is implemented successfully. The model has five elements or building blocks that all need to be in place for change to be successful.

A	Awareness of the need for change.
D	Desire to support and participate in the change.
K	Knowledge of how to change.
A	Ability to implement required skills and behaviors.
R	Reinforcement to sustain the change.

The publication *ADKAR: A Model for Change in Business, Government and our Community* presents each element and the interventions that can be made to influence each element e.g. increase awareness, increase desire etc. There is also an ADKAR® assessment that can be used to identify barrier points to change so that targeted tactics can be put into action.

This assessment can be used throughout the life of a change to assess progress and to diagnose gaps in the change management activities. The results extracted from the data of an ADKAR® assessment are:

- The barrier point to the change for the organization overall.
- Specific details that will help lead to resolution of key obstacles.

There are various ways of using the ADKAR® model and collecting data. These include:

- Surveys (one-off surveys, pulse surveys)
- Focus groups

- Interviews
- Workshops.

Other methods to collect data include:

- Assessments
- Observations
- Tests
- Performance evaluations
- Performance metrics.

Each method has its advantages and disadvantages, and no one method is ideal in isolation. Therefore, good practice is to use a combination of methods to collect data that provides a holistic picture of change management progress and success.

Data that can be collected to inform change management decision-making include:

- Adoption effectiveness
- Usage and utilization
- Compliance and adherence
- Employee engagement
- Employee feedback
- Requests for support
- Issues log
- Training participation numbers
- Training effectiveness surveys.

Change readiness is a critical factor to be measured prior to any transition to implementation. See section Inventory.

A key guide to the selection of the right metrics and measures is to answer this question: what does success look like?

Let's get digital

There are more real-time employee survey tools available that can replace the old-fashioned employee opinion surveys. These tools can tell you much more such as variance in adoption across locations; variance in effective delivery of messages by management; and employee perception influenced by other events (internal or external to the organization).

The more data that is collected before and following actions or interventions can be extremely powerful. This data can feed into a predictive model that informs you, with precision, the actions that are going to increase adoption and the success of a change.

Performance from project to project can be captured including the team composition, the change stakeholders, the implementation time frame, tools, techniques, and tactics used and so on.

As more data is collected and a reference set emerges, it will become easier to build accurate predictive models of organizational change.

The same approach could be used to create a change team. If every change leader, project manager, change agent and team member underwent psychometric testing and evaluation prior to the start of a project, the data would become variables to include as you search for a causal model on what leads to successful change.[14]

Monitor / track

Measure performance against pre-defined objectives:

- Regularly gather performance data.
- Leverage existing monitoring tools where possible.
- Be clear, transparent and consistent with metrics definition and measurement.

It is crucial to understand the success of any initiative, collection and analysis of relevant data. Ultimately, this performance data can be used to drive decisions and new initiatives.

Although data collection can be labor-intensive, it is vital for tracking the organization's progress and for clarity and transparency in communicating this progress. Development of new tools is not always necessary, as monitoring tools may already exist in the organization that will meet the required needs.

Performance monitoring is essential in demonstrating continual improvement. Performance monitoring can be used to identify and prioritize areas for improvement and to set new targets. Similarly, a lack of useful data can be a barrier to implementing change programs.

It is vital to monitor and track change progress against pre-defined objectives on a regular basis. This serves a number of purposes.

It allows for identification of areas for improvement where progress is not as expected. It also serves to help identify which areas of improvement are going to be addressed first. Resources, like time and money, are finite and, therefore, have to be targeted where the largest return on investment and value on investment is going to be achieved.

Regular monitoring and tracking may lead to a change in priorities and a redirection of resources. This demonstrates commitment to successful change and the preparedness to adjust a course of action if necessary.

It allows early determination of whether the right objectives and metrics are in place. Objectives and metrics can be defined, and the data gathered, but if the data is not analyzed on a regular basis, there is no confirmation that the metrics are providing the information needed to determine the progress and success of a change.

Regular monitoring and tracking also allows timely intervention when progress toward change success goes off track. There may have been steady progress toward change success over a number of months, but this may suddenly vary due to unforeseen circumstances, which could be internal or external to the organization.

If regular monitoring and tracking are not taking place, variations may not be detected in a timely manner so that action can be taken to get the change back on track.

Report

Document performance and progress:

- Implement a corporate reporting system.
- Publish internal and external performance reports.
- Report on progress, addressing previously set goals.
- Report on future plans and commitments.

Reports communicate an organization's progress and future commitment toward change. They serve as a public record of an organization's goals and encourage transparency and accountability.

These reports also maintain dialogue with many stakeholders including employees, shareholders, customers, business partners, suppliers etc. throughout the organization.

A report can also be used for internal purposes such as establishing commitments and holding departments publicly responsible. This can be an important driver of change performance.

Reports should be clear, unambiguous and easy to understand. They should also be appropriate for the intended audience e.g. detailed reports versus summary reports.

Consider increasing the level of detail as you move from strategic to tactical to operational audiences. Use graphics for clarity and visual impact but keep it simple. The message should not get lost through overuse of inappropriate diagrams and graphs.

Reports should be created with careful consideration as to their purpose and the information that is required to be contained within the reports.

Before starting to create a report, it is important to understand the following:

- Who is the target audience?
- How will the report be used?
- How will the report be created?
- What is the required frequency of the reporting?
- What will be the content?
- Who is responsible for its creation?
- What is the expectation of the readership?

It is important to understand your target audience. Executive reporting should be short and concise with linkages to additional information, if it should be required.

The format and medium should also be considered and tailored for different audiences. Some recipients may prefer graphic representation of information and the report delivered to the desktop via e-mail. Others may prefer a textual presentation of the report content and the report made available on the intranet. It is useful to develop a reporting matrix, which is similar to the communication plan template that was discussed in section Communicate.

Who? (audience)	What? (content)	Where? (medium)	When? (frequency)	Why? (objective)	How? (responsible)
Executive	Portfolio status	E-mail	Monthly	Provide summary of portfolio / project status. Trends and actions.	Portfolio manager
Project Office	Portfolio status by project	Intranet	Fortnightly	Portfolio by project status. Trends and actions.	Portfolio manager
Project managers	Project status	Intranet	Weekly	Detailed project status against success criteria.	Project management officer
Business units	Project update by business line	E-mail	Monthly	Summary of project status by business line.	Project management officer

Table 13: Example of a reporting matrix

When producing reports, ensure it is clear what the report is about. Provide a clear and unambiguous report title and overview. In addition to statistics, facts and figures provide some commentary on the findings related to the statistics.

Discuss any trends identified, any areas for concern and any achievements that have been identified and what led to them. Include details of any actions that are going to be taken to resolve unsatisfactory results and those that are to be taken to retain and build on satisfactory results. It is important to put some context around what is being presented so that it is meaningful and adds value for the audience.

Verify / Audit

This category involves more formal evaluations than the previous category (Assess).

Practices in this category examine an organization's systems, processes, projects or products for reliability, accuracy, adherence to standards and compliance.

An audit will scrutinize operations, systems and procedures to check whether they meet external or internal standards. This not only drives improvement but also signals an organization's readiness and commitment to meeting its obligations. An additional layer of scrutiny is gained from third-party verification.

Verify

Engage an outside party to compare the organization's activities with corresponding specifications or requirements:

- Engage third-party auditors to conduct performance verification.
- Engage third-party auditors to conduct report-content verification.

Third party verification involves hiring independent auditors to conduct assurance assessments on an organization's systems, processes, projects or products. Assessment is carried out against a set of specifications or requirements documented in a standard, policy or code of practice.

External audits are increasingly viewed as important for credibility.

The external audit is similar to that described in section Audit (below) but it is conducted by external auditors. Although they are potentially more expensive than internal audits, they do provide an independent, professional and objective view of policy, processes, systems, projects, products and procedures.

If the organization is subject to standard accreditation such as ISO/IEC 20000 or ISO 9001, the use of a certified body to conduct an audit is mandatory for the maintenance of the accreditation.

If the organization is not subject to any standard accreditations, it may still wish to conduct an external audit for credibility purposes.

A schedule of regular internal audits combined with annual external audits is a good combination to ensure that the policies, processes, systems, projects, products and procedures are effective and efficient and that there is compliance and conformance.

Audit

Organizational members examine their own systems, processes, projects or products for reliability, accuracy, adherence to standards and compliance:

- Conduct regular internal audits of systems and processes.
- Create audit committees or departments.
- Ensure that the internal audit function reports to, or is represented at, a senior level within the organization.
- Draw upon existing expertise e.g. financial or health and safety auditing.

In order to move from a reactive state to a proactive state, an organization must set its own high standards for systems, processes, projects or products, and regularly check for adherence. Organizations can draw upon expertise within their organization for financial auditing or health and safety auditing to develop a robust system of sustainability audits.

Auditing is important for achieving continuous improvement and as a process of assurance to demonstrate the quality of performance against stated objectives.

Internal audits can reinforce procedures, reveal lapses and spark new momentum for ensuring change performance.

Embedding a change into the organizational culture can be assisted by the regular auditing of the organization's change programs by trained internal staff from a department dedicated to measuring performance effectiveness, making use of validated tools adapted from related industries.

It is important that systems, processes, projects or products are audited on a regular basis.

Organizations can conduct internal audits on their own systems, processes, projects or products to determine the extent to which they are adhering to specified standards.

It also serves to demonstrate the effectiveness and efficiency of the organization and the existence of internal controls.

Basically, the internal audit checks the organization is doing what it says it is doing.

An internal audit can be conducted at any time but could be triggered by a regulatory authority requiring evidence that an internal audit has been conducted; a previous audit indicating that a follow-up audit was required; a change in policy or procedures, technologies or tools, or organizational / management structure; or the need for an audit to be conducted based on the defined and agreed frequency.

If the organization has an internal audit department, then it is recommended that those resources be used to conduct the audit. Otherwise, provide some key business personnel with internal audit training so they can conduct the audits themselves. Make sure there is not a reliance on one or two people. Try and spread the load by having a number of people trained in the conduct of internal audits.

The first step in conducting an internal audit is to select the audit team including nomination of a lead auditor. Agree on the objectives and scope of the audit e.g. all policies, processes and procedures or a selection. Plan the audit schedule and which teams and individuals will need to be involved. Identify the documentation and evidence that will need to be examined.

Documentation should include:

- Policies
- Systems
- Processes
- Products
- Procedures / work instructions
- Contracts and agreements.

Evidence of compliance and conformance to the policies, systems, processes and products can include:

- Meeting agendas and minutes
- Performance reports
- Previous audit reports
- Interviews with personnel
- Observation of activities
- Analysis of systems of record
- Training records.

The audit schedule and the requirements of those involved should be communicated well in advance of the audit so that people can collate the required documentation and evidence.

The audit can then be undertaken, interviews conducted, and evidence gathered.

The policy should be examined for its objectives. Processes, systems, products and procedures should be examined to determine the roles and responsibilities, the activities that should be undertaken, and how they should be undertaken and when.

Supporting evidence should then be sought to identify the level of compliance and conformance to the specified policies, processes, systems, products and procedures.

Evidence determined as a result of interviews should be validated through more objective means e.g. physical records or data.

Where there are suspected nonconformities, these should be investigated in more detail.

The audit team will document its observations and findings and list any nonconformity that has been found. The nonconformities need to be supported by evidence and cross-referenced to the policy, process, system, product or procedure that is not being complied with.

The audit team should discuss the findings with management and staff including the evidence, observations, conclusions and recommendations to rectify any nonconformity.

Following discussion, a corrective action report should be produced that details what needs to take place to rectify the nonconformance, and by when and by whom. These reports will be input to the next audit so that a check can be made that the corrective actions have been implemented effectively.

The report should be made available to all employees in support of transparency.

The final step is to schedule the next audit that will (a) verify that corrective and preventative actions have taken place and (b) undertake an audit of a different area of the organization if a partial audit was only undertaken previously.

Building momentum for change

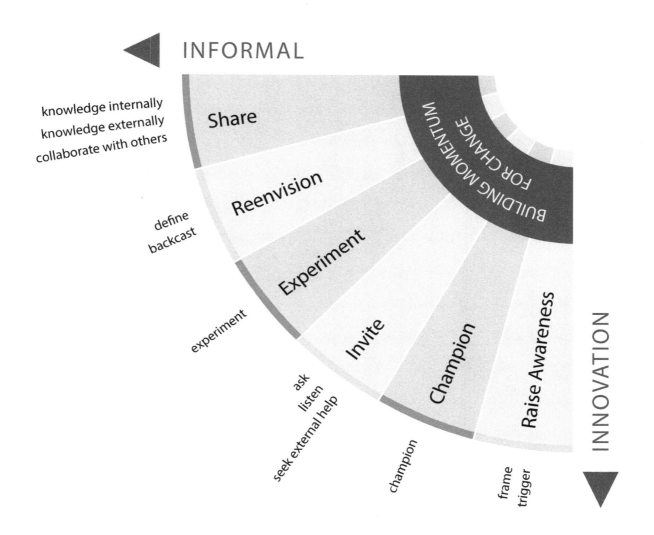

Figure 19: Building momentum for change quadrant

The preceding two sections have focused on informal and formal practices aimed at fulfilling commitments.

This section outlines several informal practices that aim to develop the new ideas and new practices needed to bring an organization closer to its long-term goals.

The practices discussed are intended to affect change by inspiring and reassuring employees to be bold and fearless as they experiment, try new things and build on each other's ideas.

The categories of practices discussed include awareness raising, championing, inviting, experimenting, reenvisioning and sharing.

There are six categories and twelve practices.

QUADRANT	CATEGORY	PRACTICES
Building momentum for change	Raise Awareness	Trigger
		Frame
	Champion	Champion
	Invite	Ask
		Listen
		Seek external help
	Experiment	Experiment
	Reenvision	Define
		Backcast
	Share	Share knowledge internally
		Share knowledge externally
		Collaborate with others

Table 14: Building momentum for change categories and practices

Raise Awareness

This category looks at techniques used to encourage or convince individuals of the importance of the change for the organization or the need to take transformative action.

These practices include triggering and framing.

Trigger

Create events that help set things in motion and disrupt the status quo:

- Disrupt people's patterns by pointing to the negative implications of current behaviors.
- Make use of visual displays to demonstrate the implications of current behaviors.
- Provide opportunities for employees to experience the implications of currently undesired behavior firsthand.
- Provide opportunities for employees to experience the implications of currently desired behavior firsthand.

Sometimes it is necessary to disrupt the status quo to generate an understanding of the need for change. Triggering is about demonstrating the risks of current thought patterns and building awareness of the benefits of alternatives.

Consider bringing visibility to current issues by disrupting existing patterns or by creating visual displays.

This could be the relocation of waste bins from offices to a central location to raise visibility of sustainability issues. It could be a visual display of the impact a lack of business continuity could have. When Google wanted its staff to eat healthier food and educate them in the process, it changed the flow of traffic through the cafeteria. Using the notion that people tend to grab what they see first; they stationed the salad bar in the front of the cafeteria. The idea, based on the theory of behavioral economics, is that if the first thing you pass is the vibrant salad bar, you will fill your plate with produce and then go lighter on everything else.

Visual displays should be concise and be created while considering the power of 'one'. Posters showing ten values and ten desired behaviors will not have an impact. When you have 20 priorities, you have none. There is a need to focus on one desired behavior at a time in order to affect change.

If you are looking to paint a picture, make it a vivid one. A great example is that of Jamie Oliver who wanted to change the eating habits of children at a US school. He got their attention with a single, disgusting image—a truckload of pure animal fat.

Wherever possible, use pictures that tell stories, and metaphors that paint a clear image of where we are now and where we want to be.

Raise awareness among the senior leadership, by providing opportunities for them to experience the negative effects of current operations firsthand.

Placing employees in face-to-face situations with those who will be most affected by their work can powerfully impact attitudes.

Triggering episodes are important for altering perceptions about the implications of current practices. Interventions 'mid-action' can provide employees with tangible evidence that different behaviors are required to achieve superior outcomes.

The use of experiential learning tools such as simulations are good techniques for raising awareness, experiencing the impact of good and bad practices, and providing employees with opportunities to work face-to-face with those most impacted by their processes, practices, products etc.

Many organizations use experiential learning techniques such as simulations to demonstrate the implications of undesired behavior and desired behavior.

Experiential learning can be defined as the process of practically engaging learners in an authentic experience that has benefits and consequences. Experiential learning can generate an understanding of the need for change by creating that 'a-ha' moment when everything suddenly makes sense and the need for change becomes clear. It allows the participants to make mistakes in a safe environment and it can break down silos encouraging cross–departmental collaboration and communication.

Simulations use gaming dynamics to mirror the real world internal and external to an organization. They can demonstrate the need for alignment through the setting of shared goals and accountabilities.

Most simulations are based on the iterative learning cycles described by David Kolb in his book *Experiential Learning*. Kolb suggested that there are four stages of experiential learning.

Stage one is 'concrete experience'. This is where a group of people participate in a practical exercise. Learning is obtained from specific experiences and it relates to people. This stage is about 'feeling'.

Stage two is 'reflective observation'. This entails observing before making a judgment by viewing the environment from different perspectives. This could take the form of discussion and feedback or individual reflection. This stage is about 'watching'.

Stage three is 'abstract conceptualization'. This stage involves the logical analysis of ideas and acting on intellectual understanding of a situation. This is where sense of the situation is made and may involve the input of an ITSM practitioner to assist in the process. This stage is about 'thinking'.

Stage four is 'active experimentation'. This stage is concerned with the ability to get things done by influencing people and events through action. It includes risk-taking. This is where the participants determine how they are going to put what they have learned into action. The experience, observations and analysis, along with practical and theoretical input are brought together and the participants attempt to predict what will happen next. This stage is about 'doing'.

Generally, in simulations, a series of rounds are played out, each intended to enable the participants to progress their fictional organization through various levels of maturity.

The first round is often chaotic due to a lack of policy, processes, systems and procedures. There is little collaboration and communication between the various functions and roles, and this often results in the organization moving backwards instead of forwards. Customer satisfaction is down, and the organization is losing money.

As the game progresses, the participants experience how system and process improvements that span the organization can help achieve performance targets and corporate profitability.

By the final round, a high level of maturity has been reached and the organization is in a far better situation than it was at the end of the first round.

The participants are now able to take away the lessons learned from the simulation and apply them back in the workplace. There will be an understanding of the impact of their function, role and activities on the achievement of the organizational goals and objectives.

There will be a far better understanding of the implications of undesired behavior and implications of desired behavior.

Frame

Construct and present a fact or issue from a particular perspective:

- Frame the change as a financial opportunity or put it in quantitative terms.
- Frame the change in everyday business language.
- Frame the change as urgent.
- Consider framing the change as innovative or 'cutting edge'.
- Consider framing the change as being about quality.
- Consider framing the change in terms of maintaining a license to operate.
- Consider framing the change as good publicity and contributing to reputation.
- Consider framing the change as 'the right thing to do'.
- Consider framing the change in terms of its benefits for employees.
- Avoid emotional language.

It is important to stress the importance of a change in ways that reflect the organization's values and in a language that aligns with organizational priorities. Where possible, tie arguments to money and convert ambiguous terms into a language that will resonate with the audience. Messages may need to be tailored differently for different audiences in the organization, but it is important to remain authentic when doing so.

Framing a change as a financial opportunity and using simple everyday business language (such as win-win or cutting edge) is key to successful championing. Framing the change as urgent also increases the likelihood of success. The inability to generate a sense of urgency can be a prime cause of change failure.

Where possible, the change should be first framed as having high financial payoff. Then, more framing dimensions tailored to the distinctive priorities of the target audience can be added e.g. how it contributes to innovation, how it is relevant to corporate values, how it will increase customer satisfaction, how it will increase employee engagement, and how it will generate good publicity.

Unlike appeals to the general public, dramatic and emotional language is not as effective as a business case framing when discussing change within companies (exceptions may occur when the organization already has a strong change culture).

Issues are more likely to lead to change if they are framed as concerns. Frames that pick up on organizational values or organizational priorities and use organizational language will be better received. If an issue does not fit with organizational values, it will not reach the organizational agenda.

Choosing the right words is extremely important to mobilize internal support. Terms like 'quality management' and 'continual improvement program' can be loaded and viewed as jargon.

Note that businesses can avoid these terms altogether and still be 'leading edge' by ensuring that their actions clearly and consistently demonstrate a commitment to quality and continual improvement.

Whenever possible, the change should be framed in business terms that resonate with the organization and, where possible, tie arguments to dollars.

If the organization is at an early stage along the change continuum, consider avoiding terms like quality management and continual improvement altogether. Layered upon this core framing, champions may also wish to tie the change to other strategic priorities or conversations being undertaken in the organization. Stress the urgency of addressing the change but avoid emotional language when doing so.

Tailoring messages to suit different audiences in the organization can be effective, but it is important to remain authentic.

Leaders of change may consider talking to those impacted by change about reframing.

Reframing is when you are able to look at a situation in more than one way. When we experience an event; we generally make an initial assumption and interpretation of that event. This is a frame.

When we reframe, we look at the event from different perspectives. We take a situation observed from one angle and view if from another angle to give it more context. This is a reframe.

The act of reframing looks to remove negativity from the perspective and increase the positivity by looking for opportunities.

A great example of reframing is the story of Tom Watson, the founder of IBM. Watson was aware that one of his employees had made a mistake that cost the organization 10 million dollars. The employee was asked to meet Watson in his office. As the employee entered the office he said, "I suppose you want my resignation?" Watson looked at him and said in disbelief, "Are you kidding? We have just spent 10 million dollars on your education."

In this reframe, Watson recognized that the mistake had already occurred, and that the money had already been lost but the situation could be seen as an opportunity to recover some value from this employee.

Reframing forces us to be more focused, creative and innovative. It forces us to stand back and see things differently. It increases our resilience in the face of constant change.

Imagine standing on the edge of the platform in the subway. As the train comes through the station at close proximity, the velocity pushes you backward like a shock wave. It is disturbing. But when you stand farther back, the speed of the train seems much slower, and it is much less disturbing. So, depending on where you are standing—your vantage point—your perceptions of events and change can be quite different.

Reframing allows us to see something in a different way, in a context that enables us to recognize and appreciate that there are positive aspects to the current situation. Reframing allows us to take onboard whatever has happened and find opportunities rather than problems.

Reframing is not oblivious to the fact that events we encounter are often difficult, dramatic and disruptive. But rather than succumbing to them and viewing them as rejection, hardship, damaging and destructive, we can choose to reframe them.

> **"Change how you see and see how you change."** —Zen proverb

Wonder over worry

Author, Amber Rae, coined the term 'wonder over worry'. Reframing means you choose whether to see a challenge as a worry or a wonder.

Unfortunately, our brains are hardwired to give more focus to negative experiences than positive ones. This was crucial, in ages gone by, when survival was of the upmost concern while hunting for food in tiger infested jungles. Our focus needed to be on the negative experiences.

Research has shown that negative thoughts stimulate the areas of the brain that promote depression and anxiety. Positive thoughts stimulate the areas that result in feelings of calm and peace.[15]

When we reframe, we can train our brains to wonder rather than worry. We take a moment to pause, step back and reframe a situation by being curious. We can choose to allow the default mode of negativity to take over or to reframe and see things through a curious and positive lens.

Champion

This category looks at using individual initiative in advancing the change agenda.

Champion

Act of an individual (champion) to take up, support or defend a course of action:

- Build coalitions.
- Inspire others through dedication and commitment.
- Do your homework. Learn as much as you can about the area of change and how it relates to your organization.
- Consider organizing teams of change champions.

Individual initiative can be extremely powerful in advancing the change agenda.

Champions recognize the importance of the change for the organization and are able to bring the issue onto the organizational agenda.

Identify change champions and organize change champion teams. While champions can get the ball rolling, the organization's leadership will need to take up the cause to ensure progress continues. For this reason, keep a particular eye out for influential people within the organization who can build and maintain momentum.

Coalition building and inspirational appeal are two successful influence tactics. Successful champions enlist help or endorsement from others to give them added credibility.

Unsuccessful champions are those who have failed to inspire others. Unsuccessful champions also lack preparation and background research on the issue at hand.

Internal champions are more likely to be successful than outsiders.

Senior managers and board members can be particularly effective champions due to their positions and influence. While individual champions are important, it often takes a team of champions to advance the change agenda.

The appointment of a known and respected champion to manage the organization's change program is key to successfully embedding a culture of change within the organization.

Change champions are required to overcome the inertia generated by responses such as 'we have always done it this way'. Change champions will push against the inertia, the passive resistance or the outright opposition to change. They will challenge the status quo.

We need change champions to:

- Be positive advocates for change(s), and influence and change behaviors.
- Explain the 'why' for the change(s).
- Explain to employees "what's in it for me" through tailored communication.
- Quickly and regularly disseminate accurate information about the change to avoid the rumor mill spinning up and derailing the change.

- Mitigate the need for the 'noise' around change (e.g. rumors and speculation) and maintain productivity.
- Gather feedback and monitor and track readiness for change.
- Coach and mentor people though change(s) and help them deal with uncertainly and ambiguity.
- Be a local 'go-to' person for employees when they want to ask questions, give their opinions, express their concerns etc.
- Be empowered to take action to resolve issues and concerns without waiting for hierarchical endorsement.

Change champions at any level of the organization need the following skills and competencies:

- Communication
- Listening
- Influencing
- Empathy
- Emotional intelligence
- Problem-solving
- Networking
- Patience and perseverance
- Motivation
- Coaching
- Facilitation
- Business acumen.

When selecting change champions, in addition to them possessing the above skills and competencies, they should be:

- Well-liked and respected by their peers
- Well-connected
- Collaborative
- Flexible and courageous
- Passionate and driven
- Charismatic and influential.

Where necessary, we need to equip change champions to be the best they can be in the role.

In addition to training to address any skills and competency gaps, it is useful to have a ½ day or 1-day introductory session where they get to understand their role in more detail and the support mechanism available to them.

They also get the opportunity (physically or virtually) to get to know one another and how they will work together. This has to be a collaborative network.

The session can also provide education around change management including key principles of the psychology of change, stakeholder engagement, sponsorship, impact and readiness assessments, resistance management, training needs analysis, and reinforcement techniques etc.

Invite

The practices in this category reflect attempts to solicit and be receptive to ideas and input from employees and others outside the organization.

These practices range from inviting input to showing genuine interest in employees' opinions and ideas to being attentive to their suggestions and recommendations.

The practices in this category are asking, listening and seeking external help.

Ask

Proactively seek opinions and ideas about how to grapple with issues:

- Encourage dialogue and questions.
- Hold staff meetings to generate ideas for change.
- Request feedback from internal and external stakeholders.
- Bring in external consultants to hold employee feedback sessions.
- Allow anonymous feedback (suggestion boxes or online mechanisms).
- Ask open-ended questions to generate talk about change.
- Ask employees how they would like to improve things in an ideal world.
- Ask employees if they are proud of their organization.

As an organization develops and changes, employee and other stakeholder feedback becomes a vital input to the innovation process. There are many ways to proactively garner feedback: host staff meetings, conduct surveys, create suggestion boxes. Employees and other stakeholders can be prompted to voice their opinions on the organization's strategy, suggest new and creative ideas and solutions, and join open discussions about issues.

Create a safe place for bold ideas to emerge. Organizations can ask employees how they want the organization to be perceived by others. Encourage employees to volunteer their feelings about the organization. Ensure that everyone's opinion is counted and that feedback from employees is seen as the norm by management. Senior leadership should solicit opinions so that employees feel heard.

Integrate change into the organizational culture by holding regular (e.g. quarterly) meetings at which employees address core values and are encouraged to voice their opinions about the organization's business and vision.

Garnering opinions and ideas should not be limited to employees. The opinions and ideas of supplier and partners, and customers and consumers should also be sought. These entities can have different perspectives of change(s) and valued insights.

It can increase employee feedback if innovative ways of encouraging and collecting that feedback can be utilized.

Making employee feedback visible across the entire organization can be extremely powerful. Transparency is key to great employee engagement. A dashboard that allows all employees to see where their colleagues' feedback is coming from, can send a powerful message.

This includes the organization being transparent about what employees are saying and demonstrating intent to address the most pressing issues.

This can encourage more employees to contribute their feedback.

The downside to this approach occurs when the organization fails to address the issues of most importance to employees. Credibility and trust are soon lost.

Organizations could leverage the idea of question walls. Often used in schools, a question wall is a space where students can write down their questions. A question wall is made by covering a wall with butcher paper or chart paper. The power in this approach lies in the type of questions written on the wall as it indicates (a) what employees want to know and (b) the information they need clarified. Many organizations digitize this approach and provide an interactive question / feedback wall where every employee can ask questions or suggest ideas through various devices at any time.

Gamification is an area that can have significant impact on gathering employee questions, opinions and feedback. Employees play a game, in a digital environment, that offers points, status and rewards as they provide feedback, ask questions and share their opinions in regard to change(s).

The theory is that everyone likes games, and that we all like a bit of friendly competition and the rewards that come with it.

Listen

Be receptive or open to opinions and new ideas:

- Provide opportunities for employees to speak to senior management.
- Listen more and talk less.

When attempting to bring about change, organizations often make use of the proactive behaviors already described in this section. But, while it is important to raise awareness, champion and even solicit opinions by asking, it is equally important to listen.

Some of the best change programs are based on input from employees in operational departments; these employees are ideally situated to make recommendations on improving systems and processes if senior management is willing to listen. In fact, employees may find the ear of senior management just as rewarding as monetary incentives.

Listening to an employee helps them to feel valued and helps to create shared meanings.

Corporate effectiveness in developing responses to concerns and implementing improvement is influenced by an organization's willingness to listen to stakeholders.

If we don't listen effectively, we cannot respond appropriately.

Effective listening is critical to understanding employee perception. Effective listening can avoid misunderstanding, which in turn, leads to avoidance of conflict. Misunderstanding and conflict have no place in the workforce.

Effective listening helps us to avoid jumping to unfounded conclusions and making assumptions.

When we are under pressure and feeling stressed, it is easy to listen with emotional barriers in place and not really hear what is being said. Our emotions and unconscious biases can get in the way. These can translate what is being said into something quite different.

In a stressful environment brought about through constant change, it can be easy to become distracted by what is going on around you and not hear a conversation in its entirety.

Effective communication and effective listening go hand in hand but as the saying goes, "We have two ears and one mouth for a reason." This means we should use them in that proportion—we should listen twice as much as we speak.

Seek external help

Solicit input from those outside the organization to find ways to improve internal practices, processes or systems:

- Bring in industry experts to provide training or assistance with issues and change.
- Get guest speakers to talk about issues and change.
- Consult with suppliers or customers for ideas.

Seeking external help exposes the organization to new ideas. Industry associations can help companies deal with the complexity of issues by providing practical guidance.

Outside consultants can offer training and systems or provide insights into what other organizations are doing.

When looking for new ideas, consider consulting customers or suppliers. Valuable information can be gained by asking customers for assistance. Turn to external experts to find ways to learn from their knowledge and capabilities and then transfer them internally.

Outside consultants can bring important resources, as they are skilled at suggesting which practices can be implemented in order to bring about the desired improvements.

While looking inside the organization to find ways to improve, there is always the danger that we have a narrow or limited view. We can look to other organizations that have solved a similar problem in a different way from the one we are currently pursuing.

We can source external help by attending industry events, professional association meetings and conferences. These are excellent opportunities to network, and gather and share information. Attendance at these events can also provide a level of assurance when it is revealed that the approach to change(s) being taken within the organization have been successful in other organizations. There is positive reinforcement of the approach which can be shared back in the organization.

Experiment

Practices in this category explore ways to support the development of new ways to do things.

Experiment

Encourage employees to try new things or develop their own solutions:

- Encourage research and experimentation that is aligned with the company's values.
- Provide autonomy to workers and managers to develop new solutions to challenges.
- Allow self-started projects to germinate.
- Allow employees some flexibility with regard to implementation.

Innovation requires an organization that encourages employees to challenge the rules. Some of the most creative ideas result when employees are given flexibility to try out new ideas. This will also increase engagement and result in a shared learning process.

Managers can spur innovation by allowing employees the autonomy to solve problems in their own way and by leaving flexibility for implementation of objectives. Managers could be given the freedom to implement programs without sign-off from their parent company—as long as the programs are consistent with corporate objectives and values.

Change can be most successful when mixing short- and longer-term goals and then allowing employees flexibility in how they achieve those goals. Employees should be given resources that allow them to test and evaluate ideas. This approach provides management control over the process while also building a culture of free and creative thought.

Proactive companies create an environment that fosters experimentation and new ideas related to change by allowing managers to use their discretion and by encouraging employees to respond to new opportunities. This results in both a change in culture and organizational capabilities.

Setting an innovation challenge for the organization can foster a learning culture. Employees can be encouraged to conduct many experiments to meet the challenge and, more importantly, learn how failures cause the organization to shift strategy in order to overcome the dilemmas standing in the way of meeting the challenge.

All change journeys will require new and different ways of doing things.

Welcoming, supporting and encouraging experimentation can help create a culture of change and innovation. Organizational leaders need to encourage new ideas by being supportive of trial-and-error and experimentation, and allowing employees a certain degree of freedom in deciding how to achieve change goals and targets.

This means that while being prepared to experiment, everyone needs to embrace the vulnerability that this brings, and accept that there will be mistakes and recovery from failure. It is okay to jump into the unknown. It is okay to take risks.

Innovation is now key to organizational survival and innovation is fueled from experimentation. You cannot change things for the better if you are not prepared to experiment. Everyone has to be prepared to fail along the way. Failure is a way of learning what doesn't work and what does. If you accept failure, you can move forward.

There are endless stories of innovation failures from organizations and people who are extremely successful. They are successful because they were prepared to experiment. Examples of failure include Apple III, Google Wave and Microsoft Zune but yet these organizations thrive. 3M experimented with glue, which was a failure because it didn't stick, but that failure led to the basis for the Post-it® Note, which became a huge success.

Recognizing failure as a learning process has led to the word 'fail' being used as an acronym for learning and resilience. These include:

- First Action in Learning.
- First Attempt at Learning.
- Forever Acquiring Important Lessons.
- Found Another Interesting Lesson.
- Future Always Involves Learning.

Experimentation happens when we think outside the square and look at things from a different perspective. This could mean taking a walk in someone else's shoes. It could be a customer, consumer or colleague. We might want to look at how their experience could be improved. What experiments could be undertaken to determine the best way to improve that experience?

Reenvision

Periodically, organizations should step back from everyday operational issues and think holistically and prospectively. Reenvisioning involves determining what the change means to the organization and how this impacts the next steps toward embedding the change. It also involves developing a new conception of how the organization could or should operate or imagining an ideal future state for the organization and allowing this vision to drive current actions.

The practices covered here are defining and backcasting.

Define

Develop an agreed upon definition of the change for the organization:

- Involve multiple stakeholders in defining the change.
- Ensure that the definition of the change is consistent with the organization's values.
- Regularly reassess whether everyone has the same understanding of what the change means for the organization.

It is important to define what the change means to the organization and ensure that all employees and other stakeholders have a common understanding.

Encourage discussions between managers and senior leaders to agree on a clear definition of the change.

Solicit input from internal and external stakeholders to establish an agreed upon definition of the change that is relevant to the business. Choose a definition of the change carefully, because it can shape and influence employee behaviors. Continually ask whether the change is defined well enough and whether everyone interprets it in the same way.

Regardless of the size or scope of the change, a clear and compelling definition is key.

When change is constant and ever increasing in speed, this step can often be overlooked in the desire to get the change happening.

Imagine that you want to extend your home and add on two rooms. You would not engage builders to start work without first having a clear plan of what the change will look like. The same applies in the organization. There needs to be a shared understanding of what is changing, why it is changing and what impact the change will have.

There has to be a clear picture of the destination. Why would you set out on a journey with no idea of where you are going? If you don't know where you are going, how do you know how you will get there? If you don't know what the destination looks like, how will you know when you have reached it?

It is also important to know what behaviors have to change in order to reach the destination. What is the current state and the future state and how is the gap going to be bridged?

The key questions to be answered when defining change are:

- Why are we changing?
- What is changing?
- What happens if we don't change?
- What will success look like?

Backcast

Envision a different future and identify the actions required in order to reach it:

- Imagine a desired future.
- Work backwards from the future vision to determine the necessary steps to get there.
- Set distinct milestones to help construct the path to the future.

Backcasting is a useful practice to ensure an alignment between what the organization is doing now and where it ultimately wants to be. It is about building a logical set of stepping-stones from the future back to the present.

Ask the big questions about where the organization should be in 10 to 20 years and start taking the necessary steps to get there. Look beyond current products and think about the value offered to customers.

Use a reverse engineering approach to develop a vision: start with the ideal and then work backwards. Imagine several alternate future states and then use them to engage stakeholders in developing the paths to achieving them. This allows the design of a future state that is informed by the past but is not an extension of it.

Backcasting allows employees to ensure they build innovation into all aspects of their work as they move forward. For example, each year employees can be asked to consider the organization, its practices and its culture, and to indicate changes that are needed to close the gap between where the organization is and where employees want it to be.

It is useful for employees to take time out from day-to-day operational issues and imagine a desired future for their team and the organization. This allows a check to be made that current change initiatives are aligned with where they ultimately want to be. It is also good to develop a vision and then work backwards. Engage all the stakeholders in determining the steps that are needed to achieve the vision.

Backcasting can take place on an annual basis. The broad steps to carry out backcasting are as follows:

- Obtain an experienced facilitator who can run an effective and efficient backcasting session. This will be critical to the success of the session.
- Find a location (or virtual environment) where there is a wall or table on which you can place a large number of sticky notes. Sticky notes of various colors and sizes will be required.
- Invite employees and stakeholders to the backcasting session. This is often easier if it is a physical meeting but if this is not possible, utilize collaboration channels such as videoconferencing etc.
- The group needs to determine how far into the future the group is going to look e.g. five years, ten years, 15 years etc.
- The facilitator will have established a set of questions to be used in the session including questions about the time frame, current state, future ideal states, actions, indicators, risks and opportunities.
- The group should identify the current state and the future ideal state. This could include the current and future consumer or customer perception. One or more possible (and successful) future states should be defined. These should not be constrained by current product, services, processes, technologies etc. The facilitator should encourage 'blue-sky' thinking.
- Each future state should be considered, then the group works backwards to identify the actions, assumptions, risks, benefits and other indicators that could lead to these future states. These are all captured on the various sized and colored sticky notes.

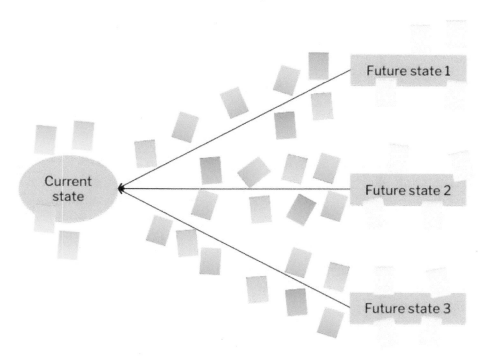

Figure 20: Backcasting example

- The outcomes should be captured and shared with stakeholders who were unable to attend the session. Their feedback should be incorporated.
- The results of the session should be captured. Use methods such as charts, maps, stories, action lists, photographs of the sticky notes etc.
- The results of the session should then be used in strategic planning sessions.
- The exercise should be repeated on a regular basis e.g. annually and aligned with the strategic planning cycle.

Share

The practices in this category focus on sharing information internally and / or externally with the aim of furthering the change agenda and working with other organizations to further a broader change agenda.

At some point, organizations on a change journey realize they are often facing issues that extend across departmental and even organizational boundaries. In trying to address organizational issues, it may help to leverage internal and external networks and incorporate a variety of perspectives. Internal collaboration will allow employees to build on each other's ideas and allow best practices to disseminate throughout the organization.

Similarly, sharing ideas and practices with other organizations can raise the performance of everyone involved.

The practices discussed in this category are sharing knowledge internally, sharing knowledge externally and collaborating with others.

Share knowledge internally

Make use of the organization's diversity:

- Encourage sharing of knowledge across different functional areas.
- Create cross-functional teams to work on issues.
- Ensure interdisciplinary representation when building working groups.
- Make use of the diversity of talents and ideas across your organization.

Changes often impact multiple areas of the organization. To understand how changes in one area may affect or even benefit other parts of the organization, it's a good idea to consult across functional areas. By ensuring diverse functional representation in working teams, the organization will benefit from a range of perspectives. These diverse perspectives will allow for more solutions that accommodate a multitude of different expectations and requirements.

One solution is to assemble interdisciplinary and cross-functional teams to collaborate on the change or consider bringing together key people from across the organization in positions of responsibility where the change can make a difference.

Mobilize commitment by cross-functional and cross-hierarchical team collaboration and establish formal senior level change teams that have the power to affect the transformation and the seniority to take accountability for it.

Link people who are working on similar initiatives across the organization to provide support and learning and to encourage innovation through collaboration.

Without deliberate efforts to coordinate, staff are often isolated and not integrated with the core of the organization and have to work hard to develop closer relationships with other employees.

The lack of shared knowledge between staff can result in misunderstandings and halt collaborative action and problem resolution. Regular formal meetings scheduled for the explicit purpose of sharing information and discussing and debating ideas contributes to an innovation-supportive and inclusive culture.

The success of any change is founded on clear and constant communication and sharing of information across the enterprise. This ensures that everyone is in the loop and can participate accordingly. Continuous communication enables collaboration, whereby, cross-functional teams can work on addressing issues and challenges.

Sharing information internally and encouraging participation aids in employee support and commitment to the success of change(s).

Constant sharing of knowledge across the organization has many benefits. In addition to increased employee engagement and motivation, it leads to an increase in active collaboration and creative problem-solving.

Share knowledge externally

Share knowledge externally:

- Participate in knowledge sharing opportunities initiated by industry associations.
- Join organizations that bring together other organizations that are grappling with the same issues.

Sharing experiences with other organizations and groups to learn more about how they are working to implement changes and solve issues has mutually beneficial outcomes.

Often, other organizations are working on addressing similar issues and asking the same questions.

Acknowledging that sharing information with competitors is not necessarily harmful is an important step. By sharing best practices and key learning, organizations can work together to generate solutions.

Organizations should engage in knowledge sharing in order to inform, confirm and validate their own internal approaches.

Identify local and special interest groups related to the area of change and encourage management and employee attendance. Identify user groups and forums and become a member at a local, national and international level as appropriate.

In section Seek external help, we discussed the advantages of sharing knowledge externally by attending industry events, professional association meetings and conferences. These are excellent opportunities to network, and gather and share information.

Attendance at these events allows sharing of experiences, challenges and opportunities with employees from other organizations.

Noting that there will be times when nondisclosure is required and competitive advantage maintained, many organizations are more than happy to share knowledge that does not cross those boundaries.

Collaborate with others

Work with other organizations to try to achieve shared goals:

- Collaborate with other organizations.
- Create organizational partnerships.
- Cooperate with external stakeholder groups e.g. industry bodies and user groups.

Making headway on implementing change and addressing issues sometimes requires more than information sharing. To achieve real progress on issues, it may be necessary to work with some unlikely partners such as competitors or industry bodies.

Organizations may form strategic alliances with user groups, or even competitors, to address complex problems. Industries can band together to develop best practices or to develop new processes. When an organization opts to take on larger challenges by working with other organizations, it can send a signal to those on the inside that management is serious about change.

Interacting with and listening to feedback from stakeholders can enable an organization to build the concerns of their customers, employees, shareholders etc. into its innovation processes.

Whatever industry sector your organization resides in, it is likely that there are industry bodies, professional associations and user forums that can be engaged for collaboration.

Organizations are often invited to participate in industry research aimed at acquiring new knowledge and skills and driving industry improvements. This may be driven by educational establishments such as universities, or professional bodies.

Organizations can also collaborate on the creation, or improvement, of industry best practice, education, frameworks and certifications. All of these can further the industry in which these organizations reside.

Product providers often have user groups in which organizations (as customers or consumers) are invited to participate and work with the provider to improve their products. This has a win-win situation for the provider and the customer organization.

There are many benefits of organizations collaborating with each other. This include (but are not limited to):

Increased brand awareness. For example, collaboration with other organizations to increase sustainability and the ethical behavior of other organizations within the sector, increases public awareness of the organization and its brand.

Overcoming challenges. An organization struggling to achieve its goals, may find that another organization can assist. Partnerships, coalitions and networks are more powerful than an organization operating in isolation.

Funding. Partnering with other organizations may increase access to grants and funding.

Sharing. Organizational collaboration can lead to the sharing of resources including knowledge and expertise.

Greater outcomes. Collaboration can result in greater outcomes as compared with each organization working on its own.

A great example of organizational collaboration for the greater good is the Genographic Project.[16]

This has been a collaboration between National Geographic, IBM, Helix and the Waitt Foundation.

The Genographic Project aims are:

1. To gather and analyze research data (including DNA) in collaboration with indigenous and traditional peoples across the world. This allows analysis to map their ancestry and, therefore, to understand human migration patterns.
2. To invite, encourage and educate the public through participation in this real-time citizen-science project, while they learn about their own deep ancestry.
3. To support scientific research and community-led conservation and revitalization.

Instilling capacity for change

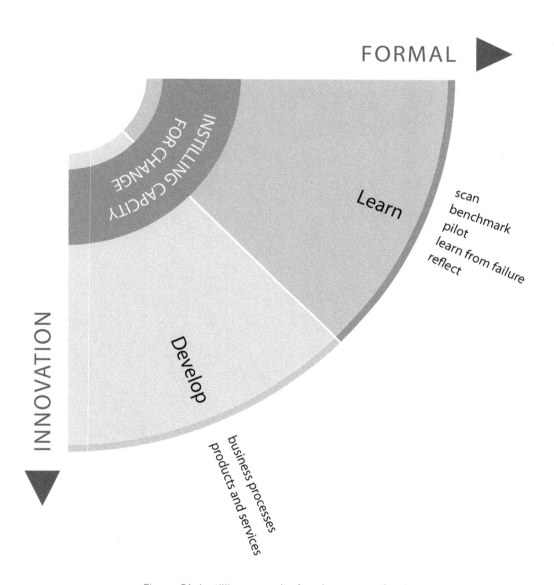

Figure 21: Instilling capacity for change quadrant

Practices in the fourth quadrant of the framework are aimed at innovation.

The practices in this quadrant take a formal approach toward building a culture that supports change and innovation.

The two categories of practices in this section can help embed continual and proactive knowledge building by institutionalizing learning in the organization (learning) and providing a foundation for future initiatives by developing formal support mechanisms for change (developing).

There are two categories and seven practices.

QUADRANT	CATEGORY	PRACTICES
Instilling capacity for change	Learn	Scan
		Benchmark
		Pilot
		Learn from failure
		Reflect
	Develop	Business processes
		Products and services

Table 15: Instilling capacity for change categories and practices

Learn

The practices in this category focus on creating processes and mechanisms to gather knowledge or skills related to the area of change.

The practices discussed here include scanning, benchmarking, conducting pilot projects, learning from failure and reflecting.

Scan

Make use of systems or processes to perceive and recognize external information:

- Attend industry conferences.
- Join a user group where members share information and best practices.
- Observe competitors' activity.
- Scan multiple sources habitually.
- Develop many diverse internal and external knowledge and opportunity networks.
- Research stakeholder needs and values.
- Scan for changes in legislation and upcoming regulatory requirements.
- Use focus groups and surveys to garner customer and employee opinions.
- Subscribe to newsletters and periodicals.
- Join online discussion forums.
- Scan social media channels for information e.g. Twitter, Facebook, LinkedIn etc.

In a rapidly changing environment, organizations must be constantly and proactively looking for opportunities and threats. Scanning entails continually looking out for opportunities. Scanning also involves researching all available sources for the latest information and expert opinions and having a finger on the pulse of a changing landscape.

Organizations should encourage employees to keep themselves up to date by accessing online information, reading books, and talking with experts to identify ways in which the organization can change.

Successful champions scan their environment, collecting information from industry conferences, consultants and competitors.

Habitually searching for new information needs to become culturally embedded in the organization so that it moves from being an individual capability to an organizational one.

The organization can routinely ask its stakeholders their opinions about its values and planned activities, which then allows it to adjust and adapt if required. Leading organizations balance internal and external focus. They build and maintain extensive links beyond their sector or industry to keep up to date with the latest practices and new developments.

There is a wealth of resources available to organizations to uncover opportunities and threats.

These include (but are not limited to):

- User forums
- Industry publications
- Internet
- Newspapers
- Magazines and journals
- Industry research, analysis and advisory services
- Social media groups
- Social media channels
- Podcasts
- Videos
- Events
- Focus groups
- Surveys
- Conferences
- Professional associations
- Consumers.

Organizations should encourage employees to scan these and other sources regularly and share information that is uncovered.

Organizations need to provide employees with the time to scan and absorb information on a regular basis as well as provide the tools to enable the effective sharing of information across the organization.

The process of an organization scanning its environment regularly to assess its development and understanding factors that can contribute to its success is called environmental scanning. This process is used to monitor both internal and external environments. Data collected can relate to competitors, industry trends, emerging technologies, and the economic and political landscape.

The results of environmental scanning are extremely useful in shaping goals and strategies. Scanning can identify the threats and opportunities that exist in an environment and, therefore, inform organizations of the opportunities it should take advantage of and the risks it should minimize.

There are synergies with a SWOT analysis as described in the section Inventory.

Organizations must scan both the internal and external environments.

Internal environmental scanning can include:

- Vision, mission and strategic plan
- Employee engagement and interaction
- Organizational structure
- Culture
- Human resources
- Physical resources
- Technological capability
- Organizational strengths and weaknesses
- Interviews and surveys.

External environmental scanning can include components such as:

- Organization
- Competitors
- Vendors
- Customers
- Intermediaries
- Trends
- Technology
- Economy
- Political and legal
- Demographics
- Environment
- Social and cultural.

The resources available for both the internal and external environmental scan are as listed earlier.

Once the organization has collected the information from the external environmental scan and the internal environmental scan, it can conduct an assessment and develop strategies to respond to the opportunities and threats as needed now and into the future.

Benchmark

Compare your business processes and performance to industry bests and / or best practices from other industries.

- Select organizational metrics that are used by others to facilitate benchmarking.
- Decide which information (if any) should be made public so that the organization's performance can be transparently compared to that of another.
- Consider benchmarking internally between divisions, business units or locations.

Benchmarking facilitates learning by situating an organization's performance relative to others. Organizations may find that they lead or lag the efforts and achievements of other organizations and can get a sense of best practices by comparing their performance to others.

When first embarking on benchmarking, see if there are existing metrics that can be adapted to the organization's purposes.

Benchmarks allow management to better measure and manage change. Internal benchmarking can help divisions set realistic targets by seeing how well their peers are doing.

Organizations embarking on benchmarking should firstly ensure there is a clear goal. The goal is not to collect a series of metrics and create a benchmark—this is just a means to an end.

The goal should be something like an improvement in efficiency of a particular process, system or service. The goal should also be business related. Once the goal is defined, it is then easier to clearly agree the scope of the benchmark activity.

There are two types of benchmarking that can be undertaken. It can be run internally using internal resources to benchmark against the performance of another organization or to benchmark against an industry best practice, framework or standard.

It can be run externally by using an external organization that would typically have pre-existing models, metrics and benchmarks that can be utilized.

For many organizations, the latter would be preferred due to the time required to develop a benchmarking model, identify comparable organizations to participate and collect the metrics across all those organizations to allow comparisons to be made.

However, if the benchmarking is taking place within the same organization and is making comparisons between different parts of the organization, then internal benchmarking may be a preferable option.

The organization should weigh up the costs of each (including the cost of building the internal capability to conduct a benchmark) and determine the most appropriate approach.

Consideration should also be given to whether this is a one-off exercise to take a snapshot of where you are today, or an ongoing activity where metrics are captured on a regular basis (e.g. monthly, quarterly, yearly etc.) to support a program of continual improvement.

Another important consideration is to determine which organizations are to be included in the study. You want to compare apples with apples and, therefore, industry sector, organizational size, geographical distribution etc. are important factors when selecting organizations to benchmark against.

Once again, this is where use of an external organization can be beneficial, as they will likely have a database of metrics accumulated over time of organizations of all shapes and sizes from which an appropriate selection can be made.

Where comparable organizations, which are capturing the metrics against what you want to benchmark, are not available then either internal or external resources will have to start contacting organizations to determine their interest in participating in the benchmarking exercise.

A common set of metrics and standardized process definitions across organizations will be required for valid comparisons. There will need to be a scalable approach for organizations of varying sizes and the information will need to be normalized so that valid comparisons can be made.

Once the results have been collected, they need to be acted upon. As mentioned earlier, collecting metrics for metrics' sake is not a goal. First, make sure you understand the results and how they apply to your organization.

Second, determine which areas you are going to focus on for improvement. Choose the areas for improvement that will have the greatest business benefit and also the quick wins i.e. those that are most easily implemented.

If an organization is ranked highly in a focused area, determine what it doing in terms of best practice and leverage from its experience and knowledge. Consult best practice frameworks for guidance on making improvements in the area being targeted.

Third, set targets. Based on where you are today, determine where you want tobe. This may be a process maturity target e.g. an increase in the maturity of a process from 1.9 to 2.75 in six months. Always remember that the increase in maturity rating must be linked to a business benefit and must not become just a numbers game.

See section Inventory.

Once you have understood the results, identified the areas for improvement and set targets, you can now create and execute an improvement plan. You have determined where you are today and where you want to be, and now you need to determine how you are going to bridge the gap.

Organizations will need to benchmark again at a later date to determine if they have achieved their goals. Allocate time to your improvement plan. Some improvements may be more easily achieved than others. Some may only take a matter of weeks to achieve, whereas others, may take months or years. So, give time for some improvements to be implemented before executing the benchmark again.

Also, use the same benchmarking model that was used in the previous execution so you are comparing valid metrics to determine your level of improvement.

Finally, use the results. Share the results of the benchmark and the improvement plan across the organization. Demonstrate how the improvement plan will benefit the organization and communicate progress on a regular basis. Transparency is key.

Pilot

Make a formal decision to undertake new initiatives or practices as a test or trial:

- Adopt initiatives that originated at the grassroots level as formal pilot projects.
- Welcome proposals and suggestions, and follow through by allocating resources to pilot the best ideas.
- Set internal targets for finding and executing pilot projects.

Ideas that develop at the grassroots level need to find their way into the formal structures of the organization if they are ever to become embedded as new practices. Piloting is one way of making this transition.

Organizations need to create a supportive environment that allows for new ideas to be given the chance to germinate, be prototyped and be implemented.

Pilot programs are important to stimulate ideas and feedback. Organizations should select areas where the conditions are favorable for successfully incubating new solutions. Organizations should create structures and allocate separate funds to allow internal entrepreneurs to build and incubate new ideas.

Setting targets for pilot projects is a way to encourage new ideas within the organization.

Initiating change in a single department and then replicating successful processes and practices in other areas of the organization can be effective in building the change into the organizational culture.

Where possible, piloting changes before rolling them out across the organization can be effective in embedding the change into the organization.

For example, when implementing a new customer relationship management (CRM) system, start with a small pilot sample of stakeholders.

Pick an area of the business that is keen to participate and experience the difference the change will bring about. Do not pick an area that has many existing problems but rather one that will show some early benefits and results.

Pilot with the selected business area(s). Once any issues with the system have been resolved, and the pilot has demonstrated some successes, the system can then be rolled out across the organization.

Communicate the success of the pilot and the benefits identified by the participants. The benefits experienced should be described in business language. Request the participants to provide an endorsement of the change and a confirmation of the benefits received. This type of marketing can increase the readiness and eagerness of other parts of the business to adopt the change and instill it into the organizational culture.

Perform the rollout gradually so that any issues arising can be addressed and corrective action can be taken before the rollout continues.

Allowing employees to experiment was discussed in section Experiment. The practice of 'pilot' is about taking those innovative ideas identified through research and experimentation, and providing a structure and funding to allow those ideas to incubate.

Where conditions are favorable i.e. there is limited risk of adverse business impact, employees should be encouraged to pilot their new ideas.

Organizations that demonstrate their support for new initiatives or practices in this manner will encourage others to try new things and develop solutions to challenges faced or opportunities to be seized.

In line with the practice of challenge as described in section Challenge, teams could be set targets for undertaking pilot projects to encourage new ideas. Each team could be challenged to undertake research and development that results in the pilot of one new idea every 12 months.

Learn from failure

Establish processes to gather new knowledge and skills from the analysis of past mistakes:

- Dedicate resources to investigating failures.
- Develop a process for making recommendations for improvement.
- Take advantage of failures and see them as opportunities for significant transformational and sustainable change.

Sometimes an organization will make mistakes. Whether it is a failure to execute a routine task or a miscalculation in the process of innovation, organizations need to view moments of failure as opportunities to improve and create momentum for change.

Acknowledging, dealing with, and publicly communicating a change failure can lead to an increase in the focus on the issues. Once the crisis is over, the organization can enter a phase of soul searching and learning, trying to figure out what went wrong and how they can improve.

Learning from failures should be approached by means of a non-punitive process of reporting and a procedure to determine what happened, why it happened and what can be done to prevent it from happening again. In this way, the organization can discover vulnerabilities in its systems and processes and can develop and monitor system improvements.

As the designer Alberto Alessi once said, "Anything very new often falls into the realm of the not possible, but you should still sail as close to the edge as you can because it is only through failure that you will know where the edge really is. The edge is also where real genius resides."

So, it is with change that failure will happen. The key to success is what you do with it. Any failure with change initiatives should be captured and used as learning experiences. Allocate resources to investigate the cause of failure. Document the findings for future reference.

It is important to celebrate failure, both as an opportunity to learn and to ensure that whatever mistake was made, does not happen again. It is the failure to stop and reflect on what has gone wrong that often leads to repeating the same mistake again.

Celebrating failure will encourage new ideas and innovation. A blame culture and finger pointing when something goes wrong will not encourage staff to make suggestions for improvements or take the lead on implementing improvements.

A punitive approach to failure will stifle innovation and lead everyone to simply play it safe.

Sharing and discussing failure can lead to unforeseen solutions. An example is the 3M Post-it® Note story. Dr. Spencer Silver was seeking to invent a new super adhesive. He failed. What he created was a weak compound that wouldn't hold anything together. Rather than hide his failure, he shared what had happened. Years later, a colleague of Dr. Silver with whom the failure had been shared, remembered the "light, repositionable adhesive" while daydreaming about a bookmark that would stay put in his church hymnal. Of course, the rest is history.

See section Experiment for additional discussion on failure.

Reflect

Carefully consider what the organization is doing. Ask questions about what the organization is doing and why:

- Set regular opportunities to reflect on priorities.
- Stand back and assess the macro perspective.
- Observe organizational trends and ensure these are consistent with values.
- Take a holistic view and be aware of the organization's surroundings.
- Implement formal feedback systems.
- Institutionalize time for reflection.

It is important to reflect on what the organization is doing as part of the learning processes, along with the need to create regular opportunities to reflect.

Taking one step back to reflect can be very revealing and result in two steps forward. Through regular assessments and feedback mechanisms, an organization can begin to formalize and institutionalize its process of reflection.

Organizational reflection is a process that involves spending time away from the normal work routines, whereby individuals and teams can think and reflect on what they have learned and what they can do more effectively in the future.

Employees need to be given time away from the "always on" position to reflect on what went well and what didn't go so well.

Research conducted at the technical support center of Wipro, a business process outsourcing company based in Bangalore, India, illustrated how time for reflection can increase performance.

Researchers, Giada Di Stefano, Francesca Gino, Gary Pisano and Bradley Staats, studied Wipro employees during their initial weeks of training.[17] All employees went through the same technical training but with a key difference. On the 6th day through to the 16th day of the program, some employees spent the last 15 minutes of each day reflecting and writing about the lessons they had learned that day.

The others, the control group, just kept working for another 15 minutes.

On the final training test at the end of the first month, employees who had been given time to reflect, performed more than 20% better, on average, than those in the control group.

Organizations should find ways to incorporate reflection into business-as-usual activities.

The US Army has a "lessons learned" tool called After Action Review (AAR). It is a simple and powerful tool but also a rigorous process. AARs are strictly scheduled so they don't get overlooked, and they are run by a facilitator rather than the leader of the project being reflected upon.

The power lies in the fact that anyone can do it. It doesn't need supporting technology and it gives everyone a chance to share their perspectives of what worked, what didn't work, and areas for improvement, which gives the leader powerful insights.

It can be conducted after or during an event or project.

An AAR asks the following questions:

- What was supposed to happen?
  - » The event should be divided into discrete activities, each of which had (or should have had) an identifiable objective and plan of action.

- What actually happened?
  - » The team must understand and agree facts about what happened. It is key to recognize that this is a learning exercise and not a blaming exercise. The aim is to identify the problem (if one exists).

- Why were there differences?
  - » This is a comparison of the plan with reality. The real learning begins as the team compares the plan to what actually happened and determines "why were there differences?"

- What did we learn?
  - » The team identifies and discusses successes and shortfalls.

- What improvements could be made?
  - » Action plans are put in place to improve upon the shortfalls.

- What are the things that should be sustained?
  - » Action plans are put in place to sustain the successes.

The outcomes are captured and incorporated into knowledge management so that learning experiences are shared not only across the team but across the wider organization.

The right climate needs to be created for what is often also called a "retrospective".

There needs to be openness and commitment to learning. Everyone should participate in an environment of psychological safety i.e. free from negative consequences.

A facilitator helps the team to "learn" answers and can draw out information from the participant that encourages an individual's learning as well as that of the team.

Whether it is a leader considering how their team could improve, or an employee self-reflecting on their day, it is proven that reflection is a vital part of individual and organizational growth.

Develop

This category looks at practices that create or implement new mechanisms to support future initiatives.

These practices include putting in place new and innovative systems and procedures (internal) and also products and services (external) as a foundation for future initiatives.

Business processes

Implement new internal procedures and / or systems that will support the change:

- Develop and implement new management system(s) such as quality management systems, environmental management systems, security management systems etc.
- Develop and implement decision support systems.
- Develop and implement organizational change management systems.

A management system is a proven framework for managing and continually improving the organization's policies, procedures and processes. The best organizations work as complete units with a shared vision. This may encompass information sharing, benchmarking, team working and working to the highest quality and environmental principles. A management system helps the organization to achieve these goals through a number of strategies including process optimization, management focus and disciplined management thinking.

A decision support system is a computer-based information system that supports business or organizational decision-making. The system gathers, collates and analyzes data from various sources and presents it in a manner that allows decision makers to identify problems, drive resolution of problems and make informed decisions.

When new or changed services are introduced, they will most likely result in new or changed processes and systems to support the change. For example, a financial institution looking to reduce its loan approval timescale from three months to three clicks, or an airline introducing biometric check-in, or a food outlet using drones to deliver meals—all these will result in process change.

An organization looking to improve the customer experience by providing cross-device shopping via a wide range of channels will need to provide consistency across those channels, which in turn will mean changes to processes and technologies to provide that consistent experience across all platforms.

Current processes and procedures and / or systems will need to be reviewed to determine the changes needed to support a change.

When it is determined that a change in processes and procedures and / or systems is needed to support a change, there are a number of activities to be undertaken:

1. **Mapping**. Each step of a process is mapped using tools such as flowcharts or swim lane diagrams.
2. **Analysis**. The process steps can then be analyzed to determine what steps need to be added, removed or modified to support the change(s).
3. **Redesign**. The process can then be redesigned to support the change(s). This usually takes place with those people who are directly involved with the process. There needs to be a common understanding of what the process now needs to do and then ideas can be generated.

4. **Capture**. The new process is captured and documented using tools such as flowcharts or swim lane diagrams.

5. **Implement**. The resources required to implement the change have to be acquired. A business case may be required. Implement the change along with extensive communication and training and education as needed.

6. **Review**. As the process is utilized, there should be close monitoring especially during the early stages of usage, to ensure that it is performing as expected. Where there are issues, remediation action should be taken as soon as possible.

Management systems that may be considered to support change(s) are:

Quality management system (QMS): A quality management system is focused on consistently meeting customer requirements and enhancing their satisfaction. Organizations can demonstrate their support of change and continual improvement by development and implementing a QMS. The International Standards Organization has the ISO 9000 family of quality management systems, which is a set of standards that helps organizations ensure they meet customer and stakeholder needs within statutory and regulatory requirements related to a product or service.

Environmental management systems (EMS): Any change(s) targeted at improving environmental performance can be supported by an EMS. An EMS is a system and database that integrates procedures and processes for training of employees, monitoring, summarizing, and reporting of specialized environmental performance information to internal and external stakeholders of the organization. The goal of an EMS is to increase compliance to legal standards and reduce waste.

Information security management system (ISM): An ISM describes the controls that an organization needs to implement to ensure that it is sensibly protecting the confidentiality, availability and integrity of assets from threats and vulnerabilities. It also includes risk management, a process that involves the assessment of the risks an organization must deal with in the management and protection of assets, as well as the dissemination of the risks to all appropriate stakeholders. An organization wishing to demonstrate commitment to supporting change should ensure security of all components required to support that change and others.

There are many organizational change management systems currently available to support organizations in their change endeavors. Many are focused on digital adoption and assisting with user performance support, employee onboarding and training. They can measure employee engagement levels and provide dashboards of real-time employee feedback. Some digital adoption platforms can overlay applications so that organizations can get insights into user behavior and create in-application experiences to empower users to be more productive and efficient. These leverage the power of artificial intelligence to predict and influence user behavior.

Products and services

Create new products or services that realize the organizations commitment to change:

• Develop new products and services that align with the organizational values.

In the quadrant on clarifying expectations, the integration of the change to existing products and services across the entire life cycle was discussed.

This practice is concerned with the organization's development of entirely new products and services to signal its commitment to change and its ability to stay relevant in the future.

When an organization develops new products and services that are in line with its espoused values, this can build employee pride and confidence in the organization's mission and its leaders. It can send a strong message that the organization has set new priorities.

For example, restaurant chains replacing plastic straws (as a service) with glass straws sends a strong message about the organization's commitment to changes regarding sustainability.[1]

Retailers have recently demonstrated their commitment to sustainability (and associated legislation) by stopping the provision of the single use plastic bag product in their stores.

Organizations can change how they make their products to demonstrate their commitment to their ethical values. Organizations in the clothing industry have moved their manufacturing into factories that meet the most stringent quality standards in both the clothes they make and how workers are treated.

Organizations that have a commitment to improve customer service and customer interaction could leverage technology and develop services that utilize chatbots or virtual customer assistants (VCA). A chatbot is "a service, powered by rules and sometimes artificial intelligence that you interact with via a chat interface."[18]

For example, while shopping online, you can engage in a conversation with a chatbot and mirror the type of experience you would get when you go into the physical retail store. That chatbot can ask you what you are looking for and find it for you.

New products and services such as these demonstrate the organization's commitment to upholding its values, while signaling a commitment to change and the desire to stay relevant into the future.

1

Examples of the Balanced Diversity framework in action

Guidance

The framework and portfolio approach can be used to embed any type or size of change into an organization.

The change could be a new product, system or service; a change to a product, system or service; new or changed processes and procedures; new or changed technology; a need to increase employee resilience; or a combination of all these.

Guidance on using the framework was provided in section Using the framework.

The guidance can be summed up as follows:

1. New initiative

Scan across all four quadrants and select practices from each quadrant so that a balanced portfolio approach is adopted. Selection will be driven by acquired knowledge in regard to the initiative.

2. Existing initiative

Scan across all four quadrants and identify the practices currently being employed to embed the initiative into the organization. Determine whether there is a balanced portfolio and if not, eliminate, introduce, lessen or strengthen practices until a balance is achieved. Action will be driven by acquired knowledge in regard to the initiative and its current progress.

3. Building resilience

Scan across all four quadrants and select practices from each quadrant that will increase employee resilience in the face of constant, complex and uncertain change. Selection will be driven by acquired knowledge in regard to the levels of resilience across the workforce.

New initiative

In this example, the new initiative was the introduction of a new time sheet system. The existing time sheet system was developed in house and was very basic in regard to functionality.

The new time sheet system was a time sheet app. This was chosen because much of the workforce was on the move and the app would make it easier to report time allocation. It also provided data that could be used for invoicing, billing, measuring performance and identifying time hungry activities. Most of these activities had previously been manual, resource hungry and time consuming.

It was also going to save managers time by not having to review and approve time sheets.

The project team, which comprised business personnel and end users, collected information in regard to the organization and the change.

They asked the questions contained in section Select the practices.

All the stakeholders were identified and were enthusiastic about the change. The organization was open to change. The change attributes were that it was a large change in regard to its scope but not overly complex in its implementation and application.

Having gathered the necessary information to inform the selection of practices from the Balanced Diversity framework, the project team held a selection workshop.

The project team was cognizant that there was a large number of other changes taking place at the same time and, therefore, time and resources could be limited. On the other hand, the change was generally welcomed and not a lot of effort would have to take place to overcome any resistance to the change.

The workshop scanned across each of the four quadrants of the framework and selected one or two practices from each that would have the biggest impact on embedding the change into the organization.

The choice was as follows:

Quadrant	Category	Practice	Rationale
Fostering commitment	Communicate	Tell stories	Story telling illustrated how the organization would look and feel as a result of the change.
		Customize	The messages in regard to the change were customized for different groups e.g. field staff, head office staff, payroll and managers.
Clarifying expectations	Train	Train	Different methods of training were to be utilized to meet the different learning needs.
	Assess	Monitor / track	Uptake and usage were to be monitored and tracked to identify any issues and enable early corrective action.
Instilling capacity for change	Learn	Learn from failure	Processes were to be established to gather new knowledge and skills from the analysis of any mistakes.
	Develop	Business processes	New business processes were to be developed to support the change. These included geofencing and GPS location tracking.
Building momentum for change	Invite	Ask	Employee experience, opinions and ideas were to be actively sought.
		Listen	Active listening techniques were adopted by executives and management to ensure an accurate understanding of employee sentiment.

Table 16: Example selection of practices for new time sheet system

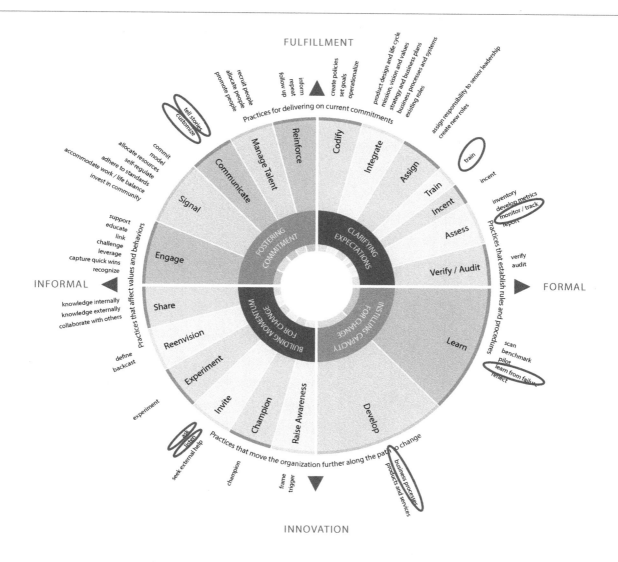

Figure 22: Example selection of practices for new time sheet system

Existing initiative

In this example, the organization has implemented an enterprise resource planning (ERP) system and associated processes. Among the many goals of the implementation was an increase in employee engagement.

Employee engagement was to be increased due to the ERP providing a more employee centric view of the workforce across the entire enterprise.

It was to improve processes and workflows across the organization and empower employees with the capability to streamline processes that had been embedded into different systems with little integration and effective interfaces. These processes included accounting, customer management, inventory and sales.

Employees would have easy and fast access to information in a single repository. They would be able to share real-time data essential to their job functions with the right stakeholder.

An employee engagement survey was conducted a month before go-live and then repeated six months later. The results were unexpected. The engagement scores had dropped by 32% over a 7-month period.

A task force was put together to determine why the ERP implementation had not had the desired effects. Some key trends emerged among the findings.

Employees said:

- They felt overwhelmed by both process and technology change.
- They were not ready for the new system.
- There was a lack of support.
- It was unclear as to what the changes meant to their roles.

The task force then set out to determine what organizational change management practices had been deployed and utilized to assist with the success of the implementation.

It convened key stakeholders including the project team and held a workshop to map the utilized practices against those on the Balanced Diversity framework.

The following was the outcome of the workshop.

Figure 23: Unbalanced portfolio: ERP implementation

It was immediately clear that the project had been run as a technology project with little or no focus on the people side of change.

A goal had been set to improve employee engagement. Business processes and systems had been integrated so they could be implemented into the ERP system. Some training had taken place. Metrics to measure both revenue increase and cost savings had been developed.

A follow-up workshop was convened with stakeholders including the project team, executive sponsors, a selection of middle management and end users.

Having identified the issues and determined the practices that had been previously selected, the workshop participants were now able to determine which practices to eliminate, introduce, lessen or strengthen to achieve a balanced portfolio.

The following actions were agreed.

Clarifying expectations

Retain **training** but increase its scope and delivery. Revised training was to include process change, job role change and ERP usage. The training was to be delivered in a variety of formats to meet the learning needs of the participants. These included face-to-face classroom training, video and computer based training, and hands on training in a sandpit i.e. safe environment.

Develop **metrics** to be retained but the metrics were to be of more use. In addition to the existing metrics, metrics to measure employee and customer engagement / satisfaction were constructed. ERP adoption metrics were also put in place.

Monitor / track to be introduced to regularly monitor progress against metrics and track trends so that timely and appropriate remediation could occur.

Fostering commitment

Support was introduced to provide employees with the ability to obtain support through open channels of communication and engagement.

Recognize was introduced to show awareness, approval and appreciation for those employees adopting the change.

Allocate resources was introduced to provide on-site expert resources to support employees in their adoption of the ERP system. The on-site expert resources acted as local super-users and the first line go-to resource for employees.

Instilling capacity for change

Reflect was introduced to allow employees regular opportunities to reflect on the reasons for the change and the overall direction of the organization.

Learn from failure was introduced to gather knowledge of the previous failures and see them as opportunities for improved change in the future.

Building momentum for change

Ask was introduced to proactively seek employee opinions, ideas and how to overcome problems and challenges. Various ways to gather employee feedback in safe environments were established.

Listen was introduced to be receptive to employee opinions and ideas. Asking is as important as listen and taking action.

Champion was introduced to identify change champions to build coalitions and inspire others to advance the change agenda.

The results of the workshop to rebalance the portfolio were as follows.

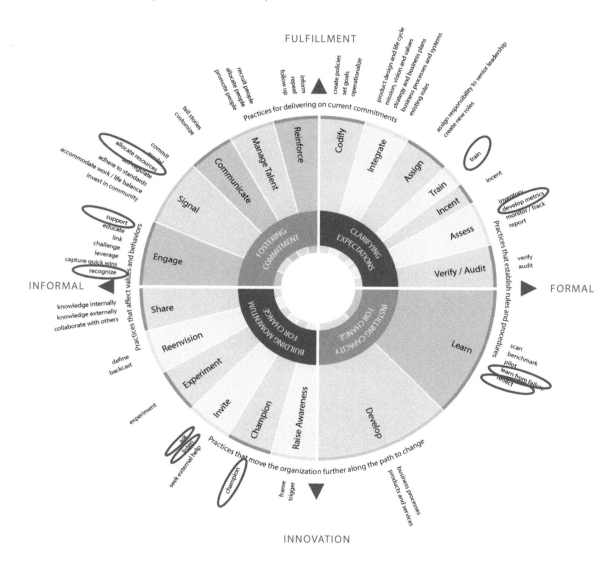

Figure 24: Balanced portfolio: ERP implementation

It should be noted that a perfect balance was not achieved nor was it necessary. Only two practices were selected from the Instilling Capacity for Change quadrant while three practices were selected from the other quadrants. We were not seeking perfection; we were seeking an overall balance.

The workshop agreed to use the Plan-Do-Check-Act approach to regularly check that the selected practices were having the desired effect, and if not take corrective action.

Building resilience

Employee resilience in the face of constant, complex and uncertain change is critical in the reduction of stress, anxiety, fatigue and burnout.

When organizations recognize that they need to address resilience at every level of the workforce, they are more likely to prevent and combat stress and burnout and build a thriving organization full of capable, productive and flourishing individuals.

Knowing which practices to select from the framework to increase resilience, requires an understanding of the current level of resilience in teams, departments, business units and the organization as a whole.

Leaders can create a "resilience dashboard" that could be populated automatically through interfaces to a resilience application that employees have on their devices, or populated manually following conversations, check-ins and pulse checks.

It is critical to remember that resilience levels can change and that high resilience today does not mean high resilience tomorrow. Therefore, resilience levels need to be monitored and tracked, and high resilience levels maintained.

There are many definitions of resilience but most talk about the ability of a person to recover, rebound, adjust or even thrive following setback, change or adversity.

I prefer to define resilient individuals as those able to bounce forward rather than bounce back. They see setbacks as possibilities to learn and they grow as a result of them. They see obstacles as challenges and problems as opportunities.

There is no single accepted set of components of resilience against which you could measure levels, but the following characteristics and situational contexts are a guide.

Measuring resilience

Self-regulation. Those who are stress tolerant and have impulse control means they respond to situations rather than react to them. They are more resilient as they have emotional intelligence. They are self-aware and emotionally aware and, therefore, can manage their feelings and stay in control.

Empathy. Empathy is the awareness of other people's feelings, needs and concerns. When we are empathetic, we improve our communication and engagement with others. We will manage difficult situations better. This lowers stress and increases resilience.

Collaboration. An important element of building resilience is reaching out to others for help and being available to help others. Working toward a common goal provides inspiration and purpose.

Exploration. Those with a growth mindset see challenges as opportunities to learn. They are curious and inquisitive. They have grit and dig deep when the going gets tough.

Realistic optimism. These people believe in change for the better but recognize that it will not just happen on its own. It requires hard work, planning and perseverance.

Humor. Having a healthy sense of humor and being able to laugh at oneself are distinct advantages in increasing resilience. Humor can be used as a coping mechanism to prepare for stressful situations.

Sense of purpose. People with a sense of purpose are more likely to be resilient. Fervent belief in a purpose means reduced chances of giving up when faced with setbacks.

Self-efficacy. Those who are confident and believe in their own abilities are resilient as a result. Self-efficacy means a person has a strong, positive belief that they have the capacity and skills to achieve their goals.

Adaptation. Flexibility and preparedness to adapt in the face of uncertain change builds resilience. Resilience comes from the ability to adapt to new ways of thinking and new ways of working, and to do so cohesively while remaining calm, attentive and confident.

Courage. Those willing to leave their comfort zone and confront their fears are more likely to overcome challenges and increase their resilience.

Gratitude. Gratitude can heal, energize and enhance cognitive thinking. It has a direct impact on focus and resilience.

While the list could go one, these are a good starting point and can be added to as needed.

In addition to the consideration of an automated or physically populated in-house developed dashboard, there are some resilience scales and measures that could be leveraged. They may, or may not, meet your needs but they are worthy of further investigation:

- Connor-Davidson Resilience Scale© (CD-RISC©)[19]
- The Resilience Scale™ (RS™)[20]
- Scale of Protective Factors (SPF)[21]
- Ego Resilience Scale[22]
- Predictive 6-Factor Resilience Scale[23]
- Brief Resilience Scale[24]
- Resilience Scale for Adults (RSA)[25]
- Academic Resilience Scale (ARS-30)[26]
- There are also models that can be employed by organizations wanting to build a resilient workforce. While no-one can be accountable for a person's resilience other than the person themselves, there are ways in which organizations can encourage the development of resilience across their workforce.
- The ABCDE Model explains how negative emotions are linked to specific experiences.[27]
- The Seven Pillars of Resilience Model helps individuals to understand the steps needed to be taken to increase resilience.[28]
- The Three Musketeers of Resilience described in the book *Restore Yourself by Edy Greenblatt presents strategies for combating personal exhaustion.*[29]

Selecting practices

Once you have acquired knowledge in regard to the levels of resilience and the components of resilience that could be improved, you are in a position to select the practices from the framework.

Let's look at a couple of examples in which we have used the Predictive 6-Factor Resilience Scale to determine levels of resilience.

The following two tables show the six domains of resilience and the components within each domain. The components that have been determined as weaknesses following measurement are highlighted in **red**. The practices that could be selected from the Balanced Diversity framework to address them are captured. It is important to note that in each example there is a balance of practices selected from each of the quadrants in the framework.

Predictive 6-Factor Resilience Scale Six Domains of Resilience		Balanced Diversity Framework		
Domain	Component	Quadrant	Category	Practice
Vision	Purpose	Clarifying Expectations	Codify	Set goals
	Goals			
	Congruence			
Composure	Regulate emotions	Fostering Commitment	Signal	Allocate resources
	Interpretation bias			
	Calm and in control			
Reasoning	Problem-solving			
	Resourcefulness			
	Anticipate and plan			
Health	Nutrition			
	Sleep			
	Exercise			
Tenacity	Persistence	Instilling Capacity for Change	Learn	Learn from failure
	Realistic optimism			
	Bounce back			
Collaboration	Support networks	Building Momentum for Change	Share	Collaborate with others
	Social context			
	Manage perceptions			

Table 17: Example selection of practices to improve resilience (1)

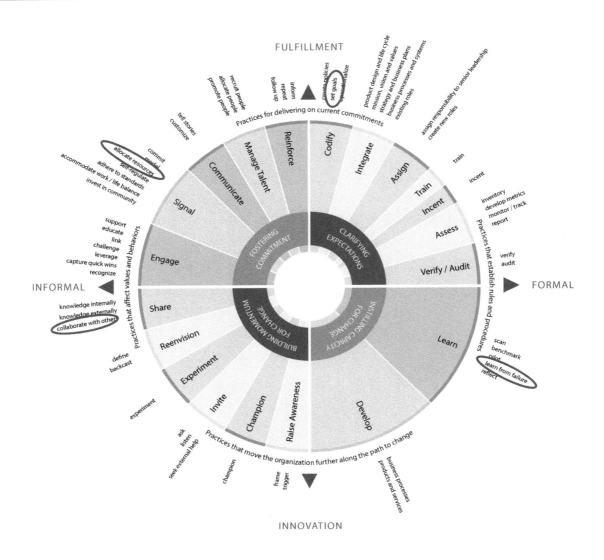

Figure 25: Example selection of practices to improve resilience (1)

Predictive 6-Factor Resilience Scale Six Domains of Resilience		Balanced Diversity Framework		
Domain	Component	Quadrant	Category	Practice
Vision	Purpose			
	Goals			
	Congruence			
Composure	Regulate emotions	Fostering Commitment	Signal	Commit
	Interpretation bias			
	Calm and in control			
Reasoning	Problem-solving	Building Momentum for Change	Reenvision	Define
	Resourcefulness			
	Anticipate and plan			
Health	Healthy nutrition	Clarifying Expectations	Train	Train
	Sleep			
	Exercise			
Tenacity	Persistence	Instilling Capacity for Change	Learn	Reflect
	Realistic optimism			
	Bounce back			
Collaboration	Support networks			
	Social context			
	Manage perceptions			

Table 18: Example selection of practices to improve resilience (2)

Conclusion

Evidence and personal experience show that a one-dimensional approach to try to embed change into an organization does not work.

There may be some immediate tangible benefits experienced but, most likely, the change will not stick. In the long term, there will be no return on investment.

The integration of change into the organization will become an increasingly uphill battle. As each successive change fails to become part of the DNA of the organization, the appetite for change will decrease. There will be increased resistance to change, apathy and change fatigue as a result of a string of failed change initiatives.

The more changes that fail, the harder it is to achieve successful ones.

The challenge of organizational change is that it involves people—the most dynamic, versatile, volatile, complex and diverse aspect of the organization. Therefore, a multi-faceted, multi-dimensional approach to change is required.

A diverse set of practices is needed—formal and informal—to deliver on current commitments as well as being aimed at innovation.

The framework within this book, used within the context of a quality improvement cycle such as Plan-Do-Check-Act, provides you with the ability to select a balanced portfolio of practices that are within your capability to execute.

It gives you the ability to reflect and adjust the selection of practices to meet the changing needs of business while always maintaining a balanced approach.

The framework alone is not a silver bullet to successful organizational change. This has to be combined with an understanding of the journey people travel when faced with change. Understanding the change curve and ensuring your change agents are equipped with the skills and capabilities to respond to each stage of the curve is a critical success factor.

Equipped with that knowledge, and the framework within this book, you can now select a diverse but balanced set of practices to embed your change into your organization—and make it stick.

Balanced diversity is how change becomes embedded into the fabric of your organization.

References

Cotter, J. P. (2012). *Leading change* (New ed.). Harvard Business Review Press.

Greenblatt Ph.D., E. (2009). *Restore yourself: The antidote for professional exhaustion* (1st ed.). Execu-Care Books.

Heifetz , R. A., Linsky, M., & Grashow, A. (2009). *The practice of adaptive leadership: Tools and tactics for changing your organization and the world.* Harvard Business Review Press.

Hiatt, J. M. (2006). *ADKAR: A model for change in business, government and our community.* Prosci Learning Center Publications.

Klob, D. A. (2014). *Experiential learning: Experience as the source of learning and development* (2nd ed.). Pearson FT Press.

Kübler-Ross, E. (2008). *On death and dying: What the dying have to teach doctors, nurses, clergy and their own* (40th Anniversary ed.). Routledge.

Endnotes

1. https://journals.sagepub.com/doi/full/10.1177/0018726715577707

2. https://www.gallup.com/workplace/236366/right-culture-not-employee-satisfaction.aspx

3. https://quirky.com/about-quirky/

4. https://ssir.org/articles/entry/using_story_to_change_systems

5. https://www.chevron.com/-/media/shared-media/documents/The-Chevron-Way.pdf

6. https://stories.starbucks.com/stories/2019/message-to-partners-from-kevin-regarding-our-mission-and-values/

7. https://www.tata.com/about-us/tata-values-purpose

8. https://hbr.org/2017/03/research-how-incentive-pay-affects-employee-engagement-satisfaction-and-trust

9. https://theirf.org/research/irf-landmark-study-uncovers-and-debunks-myths-surrounding-employee-rewards/1651/

10. https://blog.accessperks.com/2018-employee-benefits-perks-statistics

11. https://theirf.org/research/ten-things-top-performing-companies-do-differently/2229/

12. https://futurefuel.io/employee-incentive-programs/

13. https://www.dashe.com/ebooks/organizational-readiness-questions

14. https://hbr.org/2017/10/change-management-is-becoming-increasingly-data-driven-companies-arent-ready

15. https://www.collabra.org/articles/10.1525/collabra.128/

16. https://genographic.nationalgeographic.com/

17. https://hbswk.hbs.edu/item/reflecting-on-work-improves-job-performance

18. https://chatbotsmagazine.com/the-complete-beginner-s-guide-to-chatbots-8280b7b906ca

19. http://www.connordavidson-resiliencescale.com/index.php

20. https://hr.un.org/sites/hr.un.org/files/The%20Resilience%20Scale%20%28Wagnild%20%26%20Young%29_0.pdf

21. https://www.researchgate.net/publication/303161808_The_development_of_the_Scale_of_Protective_Factors_SPF_Resilience_in_a_violent_trauma_sample

22. https://psycnet.apa.org/doiLanding?doi=10.1037%2Ft01072-000

23. https://home.hellodriven.com/pr6.html

24. https://link.springer.com/article/10.1080/10705500802222972

25. https://www.ncbi.nlm.nih.gov/pmc/articles/PMC5681258/

26. http://ars-30.com/

27. http://www.centreforconfidence.co.uk/flourishing-lives.php?p=cGlkPTUyNiZpZD0xNzkx

28. https://www.skillsyouneed.com/rhubarb/7-pillars-resilience.html

29. https://www.meetup.com/en-AU/Positive-Change-mit-Appreciative-Inquiry-The-Power-of-AI/messages/boards/thread/50209290

CPSIA information can be obtained
at www.ICGtesting.com
Printed in the USA
LVHW071557051120
670810LV00011B/432